OXFORD
UNIVERSITY PRESS

fourth edition

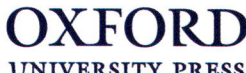

English File

Beginner Student's Book A

Units 1–6

WITH ONLINE PRACTICE

Christina Latham-Koenig
Clive Oxenden
Jerry Lambert

Paul Seligson and Clive Oxenden are the original co-authors of *English File 1* and *English File 2*

Contents

		GRAMMAR	VOCABULARY	PRONUNCIATION
1				
6	**A** A cappuccino, please	verb *be* (singular): *I* and *you*	numbers 0–10, days of the week, saying goodbye	/h/, /aɪ/, and /iː/
8	**B** World music	verb *be* (singular): *he, she, it*	countries	/ɪ/, /əʊ/, /s/, and /ʃ/
10	**Practical English** Episode 1	checking into a hotel, booking a table	**V** the classroom	**P** the alphabet
2				
12	**A** Are you on holiday?	verb *be* (plural): *we, you, they*	nationalities	/dʒ/, /tʃ/, and /ʃ/
14	**B** That's my bus!	*Wh-* and *How* questions with *be*	phone numbers, numbers 11–100	understanding numbers
16	**Revise and Check** 1&2			
3				
18	**A** Where are my keys?	singular and plural nouns, *a / an*	small things	/z/ and /s/, plural endings
20	**B** Souvenirs	*this / that / these / those*	souvenirs	/ð/, sentence rhythm
22	**Practical English** Episode 2	understanding prices, buying lunch	**P** /ʊə/, /s/, and /k/	
4				
24	**A** Meet the family	possessive adjectives, possessive *'s*	people and family	/ʌ/, /æ/, and /ə/
26	**B** The perfect car	adjectives	colours and common adjectives	/ɑː/ and /ɔː/, linking
28	**Revise and Check** 3&4			
5				
30	**A** A big breakfast?	present simple ➕ and ➖: *I, you, we, they*	food and drink	/dʒ/ and /g/
32	**B** A very long flight	present simple ❓: *I, you, we, they*	common verb phrases 1	/w/ and /v/, sentence rhythm and linking
34	**Practical English** Episode 3	telling the time	**V** the time, saying how you feel	**P** /ɒ/, silent consonants
6				
36	**A** A school reunion	present simple: *he, she, it*	jobs and places of work	third person -*es*, sentence rhythm
38	**B** Good morning, goodnight	adverbs of frequency	a typical day	/j/ and /juː/, sentence rhythm
40	**Revise and Check** 5&6			

78	Communication	92	**Grammar Bank**	131	**Words and phrases to learn**
86	Writing	116	**Vocabulary Bank**	133	**Regular and irregular verbs**
88	Listening			134	**Sound Bank**

Course overview

English File (fourth edition)

Welcome to **English File fourth edition**. This is how to use the Student's Book, Online Practice, and the Workbook in and out of class.

Student's Book and Workbook

The **Student's Book** contains all the language and skills you need to improve your English, with Grammar, Vocabulary, Pronunciation, and skills work in every File. There is an extra Culture and Reading section to help you deepen your knowledge of cultural topics and wider world events.

Use your Student's Book in class with your teacher.

The **Workbook** contains Grammar, Vocabulary, and Pronunciation practice for every lesson.

Use your Workbook for homework or for self-study to practise language and to check your progress.

ACTIVITIES **AUDIO** **VIDEO** **RESOURCES**

Go to **englishfileonline.com** and use the code on your Access Card to log into the Online Practice.

LOOK AGAIN
- Review the language from every lesson.
- Watch the videos and listen to all the class audio as many times as you like.

PRACTICE
- Improve your skills with extra Reading, Writing, Listening and Speaking practice.
- Use the interactive video to practise Practical English.

CHECK YOUR PROGRESS
- Test yourself on the language from the File and get instant feedback.
- Try an extra Challenge.

SOUND BANK
- Use the Sound Bank videos to practise and improve your pronunciation of English sounds.

Online Practice

Look again at Student's Book language you want to review or that you missed in class, do extra **Practice** activities, and **Check your progress** on what you've learnt so far.

Use the Online Practice to learn outside the classroom and get instant feedback on your progress.

englishfileonline.com

Course overview

1A A cappuccino, please

G verb *be* (singular): *I* and *you* | V numbers 0–10, days of the week, saying goodbye | P /h/, /aɪ/, and /iː/

1 LISTENING & SPEAKING

a 🔊 1.2 Read and listen.

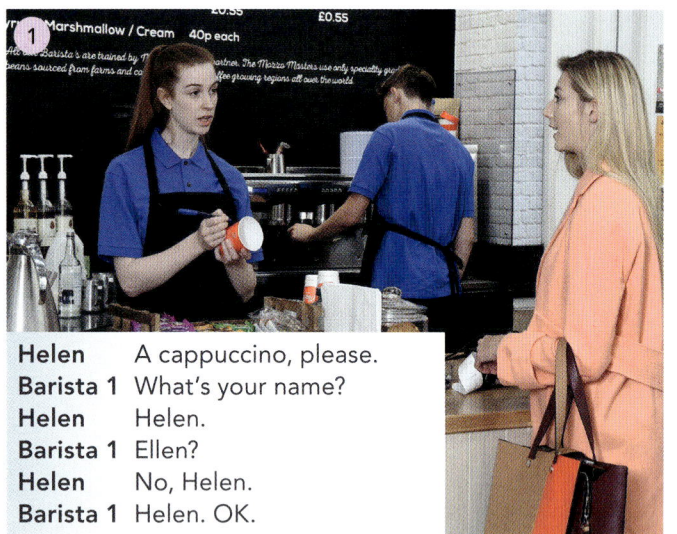

Helen A cappuccino, please.
Barista 1 What's your name?
Helen Helen.
Barista 1 Ellen?
Helen No, Helen.
Barista 1 Helen. OK.

Barista 2 Are you Diana?
Helen No, I'm not. I'm Helen.
Barista 2 Sorry.
 Helen? Your cappuccino.
Helen Thanks.

Tom Hello. Are you Helen?
Helen Yes, I am. And you're Tom.
Tom Yes! Nice to meet you.
Helen Nice to meet you.
Tom Just a minute.

Tom Hi. A tea, please.
Barista 1 OK. What's your name?
Tom Tom.
Barista 1 Dom. A tea.
Tom No, I'm Tom, not Dom.

b 🔊 1.3 Listen and repeat the conversations.

c In pairs, practise the conversations.

2 GRAMMAR verb *be* (singular): *I* and *you*

a Write *I* or *You* in photos 1 and 2.

b 🅖 p.92 Grammar Bank 1A

c 🔊 1.6 Listen and say the contractions.

1 🔊 I am (I'm

3 VOCABULARY numbers 0–10

a 🔊 1.7 Listen and tick (✓) the correct photo.

1 ☐

2 ☐

3 ☐

b **V p.116 Vocabulary Bank** Numbers Do Part 1.

c 🔊 1.9 Listen and write the numbers.

7 ☐ ☐ ☐ ☐ ☐ ☐

d 🔊 1.10 Listen and say the next number.

🔊)) one, two (three

4 PRONUNCIATION
/h/, /aɪ/, and /iː/

a 🔊 1.11 Listen and repeat the words and sounds.

🏠	house	hi hello Helen
🚲	bike	I'm nice five nine
🌳	tree	meet three tea please

b 🔊 1.12 Listen and repeat the sentences.
Hello, Helen!
Hi, I'm Mike.
Three teas, please.

5 SPEAKING

Practise with other students.

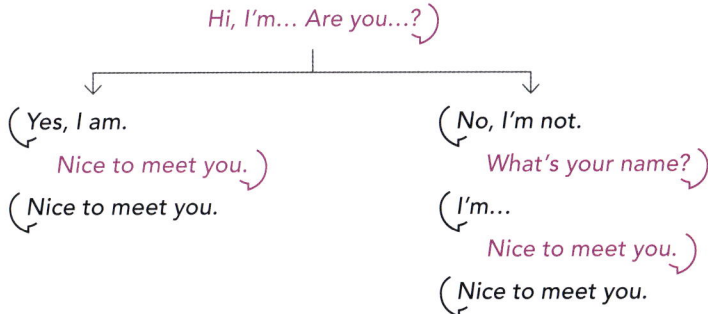

6 VOCABULARY
days of the week, saying goodbye

a 🔊 1.13 Listen and repeat the days of the week.

Monday /ˈmʌndeɪ/
Tuesday /ˈtjuːzdeɪ/
Wednesday /ˈwenzdeɪ/
Thursday /ˈθɜːzdeɪ/
Friday /ˈfraɪdeɪ/
Saturday /ˈsætədeɪ/
Sunday /ˈsʌndeɪ/

🔍 **Capital letters**
Monday **NOT** monday
Friday **NOT** friday

b Write the days of the week.
today = _____   tomorrow = _____
the weekend = _____ and _____

c Cover **a** and say the days from Monday to Sunday. What days are your English classes?

d 🔊 1.14 Listen and repeat.

Goodbye, Tom. See you on Friday.

Bye.

e Say goodbye.   (Bye. See you tomorrow.

WORDS AND PHRASES TO LEARN 1A

p.131 Listen and repeat the words and phrases.

Go online to review the lesson

1B World music

Where's he from? *He's from Brazil.*

G verb *be* (singular): *he, she, it* V countries P /ɪ/, /əʊ/, /s/, and /ʃ/

1 VOCABULARY countries

a ◆ 1.16 Listen to the music. Where's it from? Write 1–5.

☐ China ☐ England **1** Spain ☐ the United States ☐ Turkey

b ◆ 1.17 Listen and check.

c **V** p.117 **Vocabulary Bank** Countries and nationalities
Do Part 1.

d ◆ 1.19 Listen and repeat the conversation. Copy the rhythm.

A Where are you from?
B I'm from To<u>le</u>do.
A Where's To<u>le</u>do?
B It's in Spain.

e Practise the conversation with your city and country.

f **Communication** Where is it? **A** p.78 **B** p.82 Ask and answer questions about cities and countries.

2 GRAMMAR verb *be* (singular): *he, she, it*

a ◆ 1.20 Listen to the conversation. Write the countries.

A Wow! Caetano Veloso!
B Where's he from?
A He's from _____.
B Is Lila Downs from _____, too?
A No, she isn't. She's from _____.
B Is she good?
A Yes, she is. Very good.

b ◆ 1.21 Listen again and repeat.

c In pairs, practise the conversation.

d Match the words with the photos.

☐ she
☐ it
☐ he

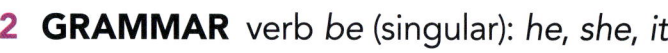

e Complete the chart for *be* (singular).

+	−
I am = I'm	I am not = I'm not
you are = you're	you are not = you aren't
he is = he____	he is not = he ____
she is = she____	she is not = she ____
it is = it____	it is not = it ____

f **G** p.92 Grammar Bank 1B

WORLD MUSIC FESTIVAL
June 18–19

FRIDAY 18 Caetano Veloso
SATURDAY 19 Lila Downs

ALSO APPEARING
Lula Pena
Mercedes Peón
Gaye Su Akyol
Sergio Mendoza
Warsaw Village Band
Martynas Levickis

3 PRONUNCIATION /ɪ/, /əʊ/, /s/, and /ʃ/

a ◉ 1.25 Listen and repeat the words and sounds.

🐟	fish	it Italy six England
☎	phone	no don't Poland Mexico know
🐍	snake	say seven city nice
ʃ	shower	she Russia

b ◉ 1.26 Listen and repeat the sentences.
  Is he from Italy?   It's a nice city.
  I don't know.   She's from Russia.

4 LISTENING & SPEAKING

a ◉ 1.27 Listen to the difference between *he* and *she*.
  1 a Is he from Egypt?   b Is she from Egypt?
  2 a He's from Turkey.   b She's from Turkey.
  3 a Where's he from?   b Where's she from?
  4 a He's nice.   b She's nice.
  5 a Where is he?   b Where is she?

b Practise saying sentences a and b.

c ◉ 1.28 Listen and tick (✓) the sentence you hear in **a**.

d ◉ 1.29 Listen and write six sentences or questions.
   1 *He's from Egypt.*

e Look at the photos. Ask and answer questions with a partner about the artists or instruments.

   Where's he from?   He's from the USA.
   Where's she from?   She's from Spain.
   Where's it from?   It's from Russia.

f ◉ 1.30 Listen and check.

g Test your partner. Point to a photo and ask a question with *Is he / she / it from…?*

   Number two. Is she from Japan?
       No, she isn't. She's from China.

WORDS AND PHRASES TO LEARN 1B

p.131 Listen and repeat the words and phrases.

Go online to review the lesson

EPISODE 1

Practical English How do you spell it?

checking into a hotel, booking a table   **V** the classroom   **P** the alphabet

1 THE ALPHABET

a ◉ 1.32 Listen to the alphabet. Repeat the letters.

**Aa Bb Cc Dd
Ee Ff Gg Hh
Ii Jj Kk Ll
Mm Nn Oo Pp
Qq Rr Ss Tt
Uu Vv Ww
Xx Yy Zz**

b ◉ 1.33 Listen and repeat the words, sounds, and letters.

🌳	tr**ee**	B C D E G P T V
🥚	**e**gg	F L M N S X
🚂	tr**ai**n	A H J K

c ◉ 1.34 Listen to the difference between the letters.

1 E A
2 E I
3 U W
4 Y I
5 B P
6 B V
7 G J
8 K Q
9 M N
10 S C
11 D T
12 W V

d ◉ 1.35 Listen. Circle the letter you hear in **c**.

e ◉ 1.36 Look at the photos. How do you say the letters? Listen and check.

1 VIP 2 CNN 3 FBI 4 BBC
5 ATM 6 USB 7 BMW 8 EU

f **C Communication** Hit the ships **A** p.78 **B** p.82
Play a game with numbers and letters.

2 VOCABULARY the classroom

a ◉ 1.37 Listen and complete the conversation with the words from the list.

Book   English   spell   What

Student	¹_____'s *libro* in ²_____?
Teacher	³_____.
Student	How do you ⁴_____ it?
Teacher	B-O-O-K.

b **V** p.118 **Vocabulary Bank** The classroom

c Complete the conversations.

1 **Teacher** _____ your books, please. _____ to page 7.
  Student _____, can you _____ that, please?
  Teacher Go to page 7.

2 **Student** _____ me. _____ do you spell 'birthday'?
  Teacher B-I-R-T-H-D-A-Y.

3 **Student** _____ I'm late.
  Teacher That's OK. Sit _____, please.

d ◉ 1.40 Listen and check.

e In pairs, practise the conversations in **c**.

f ◉ 1.41 Listen and do the actions.

1 ◉)) *Stand up.*

3 ▶ CHECKING INTO A HOTEL

a 🔊 1.42 Watch or listen to Rob. Circle a or b.

1 Rob is from _____.
  a the UK
  b the USA
2 He's _____.
  a an artist
  b a journalist
3 He's in Poland _____.
  a on holiday
  b for work

b 🔊 1.43 Watch or listen and order the sentences.

7	W-A-L-K-E-R.
	My name's Rob Walker. I have a reservation.
	Sorry?
1	Hello.
	How do you spell it?
	Walker.
	Sorry, what's your surname?
	Thank you. OK, Mr Walker. You're in room 321.
	Good afternoon.
	W-A-L-K-E-R.
	Thanks.

🔍 **Names**
name   Rob Walker
first name   Rob
surname (or last name) Walker

c 🔊 1.44 Watch or listen and repeat the conversation.

d In pairs, role-play the conversation. Use your name and surname.

🔍 **Greetings**
Good <u>mor</u>ning   » 12.00
Good after<u>noon</u>   12.00 » 6.00 p.m.
Good <u>eve</u>ning   6.00 p.m. »

4 ▶ BOOKING A TABLE

a 🔊 1.45 Watch or listen to Jenny. Circle a or b.
1 Jenny's from _____.
  a the USA
  b the UK
2 _____ is her birthday.
  a Today
  b Tomorrow
3 Locanda Verde is a _____.
  a restaurant
  b club

b 🔊 1.46 Watch or listen and complete the information.

LOCANDA VERDE
Bookings
Day _____
Table for _____ people
Time _____ (o'clock)
Name Jenny Ziel

🔍 **Z**
In the USA, Z = zee /ziː/
In the UK, Z = zed /zed/

5 ▶ USEFUL PHRASES

🔊 1.47 Watch or listen and repeat the useful phrases.

I have a reservation.   Good morning.
How do you spell it?   How can I help you?
Sorry?   A table for tomorrow, please.
Thank you.   That's right.

Go online to watch the video and review the lesson

2A Are you on holiday?

Are you American?   No, we aren't. We're from Canada.

G verb *be* (plural): *we, you, they*   **V** nationalities   **P** /dʒ/, /tʃ/, and /ʃ/

1 VOCABULARY nationalities

a Look at the photos and circle the nationality words.

b Write the countries for each photo.
1 *Turkey*   2 _____
3 _____   4 _____

c **V** p.117 **Vocabulary Bank** Countries and nationalities Do Part 2.

2 PRONUNCIATION /dʒ/, /tʃ/, and /ʃ/

a 🔊 2.2 Listen and repeat the words and sounds.

/dʒ/	**j**azz	**J**apan **G**ermany **E**gypt
/tʃ/	**ch**ess	**Ch**inese Fren**ch**
/ʃ/	**sh**ower	Spani**sh** Poli**sh** Egyp**ti**an

🔍 **Sounds**
The letter *j* = /dʒ/, e.g. **J**apan /dʒəˈpæn/.
The letter *g* = /dʒ/, e.g. **G**ermany /ˈdʒɜːməni/ or /g/, e.g. **g**o /gəʊ/.

b 🔊 2.3 Listen and repeat the sentences.
He isn't from E**g**ypt, he's **G**erman.
It isn't Fren**ch**, it's **Ch**inese.
She isn't Spani**sh**, **sh**e's Poli**sh**.

c 🔊 2.4 Listen. Say the nationality.
1 ») I'm from China. (He's Chinese.
2 ») I'm from Spain. (She's Spanish.

3 GRAMMAR verb *be* (plural): *we, you, they*

a Read the conversation. Complete it with words from the list.

American are aren't English I'm meet sit Thanks

Jessica Excuse me. Are they free?
Charles Yes, they ¹*are*. Please ²_____ down.
Jessica ³_____. I'm Jessica. Hi.
Jim And ⁴_____ Jim.
Charles Are you ⁵_____?
Jessica No, we ⁶_____. We're from Canada.
Charles Oh, OK! We're ⁷_____. I'm Charles.
Rachel And I'm Rachel.
Jim Nice to ⁸_____ you.

b 🔊 2.5 Listen and check. Then complete the chart.

be (plural)	
➕	➖
we are = we'*re*	we are not = we *aren't*
you are = you_____	you are not = you _____
they are = they_____	they are not = they _____

c **G** p.94 **Grammar Bank 2A**

d 🔊 2.9 Listen. Ask the questions.
1 ») You're Chinese. (Are you Chinese?
2 ») We're late. (Are we late?

4 READING & LISTENING

a 🔊 2.10 Read and listen to the conversation. Then number the pictures 1–5.

Jessica Where in England are you from?
Charles We're from here, from Oxford.
Jim Oxford's a beautiful city!
Rachel Yes, it is. Are you on holiday?
Jim No, we aren't, we're on business. But today's a free day.
Jessica Yes, we're tourists today! Ooh. What's that?
Jim Oh… Are they your dogs?
Charles Yes, they are. Sit. Sit!
Jessica They're very nice. But I'm not very good with dogs.
Jim Look – a free table. Over there.
Jessica Nice to meet you. Have a nice day.
Charles Thanks. Nice to meet you, too.
Rachel Bye. Good dogs, good dogs.

A

B

C

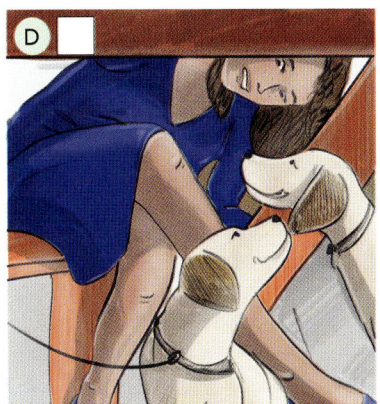
D

E

b Read the conversation again. Write short answers.
1 Are Rachel and Charles from the USA?
No, _____.
2 Are Jessica and Jim on business?
_____
3 Is today a free day for Jessica and Jim?
_____
4 Is Jessica good with dogs?
_____

c 🔊 2.11 Listen and complete the phrases.
1 Excuse me. Are they _____?
2 Are you on _____?
3 We're on _____.
4 What's _____?
5 Have a nice _____!
6 Nice to meet you, _____.

d In groups of four, practise the conversations in **3a** and **4a**.

5 SPEAKING

a Ask and answer the questions with a partner.

1 Is Pedro Almodóvar Spanish?
(Yes, he is. / No, he isn't. / I don't know.
2 Are Chow Chow dogs Russian?
3 Is Lufthansa German?
4 Is Emma Watson American?

b 🅒 **Communication** Is sushi Chinese?
A p.78 B p.82 Ask and answer about different nationalities.

WORDS AND PHRASES TO LEARN 2A

p.131 Listen and repeat the words and phrases.

Go online to review the lesson

2B That's my bus!

What's your phone number? — It's 07710 097456.

G Wh- and How questions with be   **V** phone numbers, numbers 11–100   **P** understanding numbers

1 READING & LISTENING

a 🔊 2.13 Read and listen to the conversation. Then complete the information on the card.

Pia Who's he?
Lin He's Alex. He's in my class.
Pia Where's he from?
Lin He's from Mexico.
Pia How old is he?
Lin He's 22, I think.
Pia He's very good-looking!

b 🔊 2.14 Listen and complete the conversation.

Lin   Hi, Pia. How are you?
Pia   Hi, Lin. I'm fine, and you?
Lin   I'm fine, too. This is Alex. He's in my ¹_____. Alex, this is Pia.
Pia   Hi, Alex!
Alex Hi. ²_____ class are you in?

Lin   That's my bus! Bye. See you ³_____!
Alex Bye. ⁴_____ are you from, Pia?
Pia   I'm from ⁵_____. This is my bus stop. Bye, Alex. Nice to meet you.
Alex Nice to meet you, too, Pia. What's your ⁶_____ number?
Pia   Sorry, my bus… It's 07365…!

c 🔊 2.15 Listen and repeat the conversation. Then practise it in groups of three.

2 GRAMMAR Wh- and How questions with be

a 🔊 2.16 Listen and repeat the question words.

| How | What | Where | Who |

b Complete the chart with question words from **a**.

1	A _Where_ are you from?	B I'm from Germany.
2	A _____ are you?	B Fine, thanks.
3	A _____ 's he?	B He's a friend.
4	A _____ 's your name?	B Molly.
5	A _____ 's Modena?	B It's in Italy.
6	A _____ old are you?	B 26.
7	A _____ 's your phone number?	B 07702 960836.

c 🔊 2.17 Listen and check.

d **G** p.94 Grammar Bank 2B

e Cover the questions in the chart in **b** and look at the answers. Say the questions.

3 VOCABULARY phone numbers, numbers 11–100

a ▶ 2.19 Listen and complete the phone number.

0 0   9 9 0

b ▶ 2.20 Practise saying these phone numbers. Listen and check.
1 028 901 80361
2 08081 570724
3 0131 496 0638

c Ask and answer with a partner. Write the number.

(What's your phone number?

d V p.116 Vocabulary Bank Numbers Do Part 2.

e ▶ 2.23 Listen and write the numbers.
15

f Play *Buzz*.

4 PRONUNCIATION & LISTENING
understanding numbers

a ▶ 2.24 Listen to the difference between the numbers.

1 a 13   b 30   5 a 17   b 70
2 a 14   b 40   6 a 18   b 80
3 a 15   b 50   7 a 19   b 90
4 a 16   b 60

b ▶ 2.25 Listen. Which number do you hear? Circle a or b in a. Then practise saying all the numbers.

c ▶ 2.26 Listen to the conversations. Number the questions 1–4.

☐ What's your address?   ☐ What's your email?
☐ How old are you?   ☐ What's your phone number?

d Listen again and write the numbers in the answers.
1 @ _____
2 _____ King Street
3 Age: _____
4 james_____@ukmail.com

🔍 **Email addresses**
@ = at   . = dot

5 WRITING & SPEAKING

a W p.86 Writing A form Complete an online form.

b C Communication Personal information A p.79 B p.83 Interview your partner.

6 ▶ VIDEO LISTENING Meet the students

a Watch the video *Meet the students*. Is it a nice school?

b Watch again. Circle the correct answer.
1 Alicia is in *Brighton / Bournemouth* today.
2 She *is / isn't* on holiday.
3 Rike and Hyeongwoo are *teachers / students*.
4 Hyeongwoo is *23 / 26* years old.
5 His teacher is *Stephen / Laura*.
6 Rike is *German / Swiss*.
7 Laura is a good *teacher / student*.
8 Their student house *is / isn't* near the school.

c Watch some extracts from the video. Complete the sentences with words from the list.

bedrooms big canteen computer room
garden kitchen small south

1 Brighton is in the _____ of England.
2 It's a _____ school with about 350 students.
3 His class is _____, with only five students.
4 …they're in the _____…or here in the _____.
5 It's a big house with five _____, a _____, and a _____.

WORDS AND PHRASES TO LEARN 2B

p.131 Listen and repeat the words and phrases.

Go online to watch the video and review the lesson   15

1 & 2 Revise and Check

GRAMMAR

Circle a or b.

_____ 's your name?
a Who   b What

1 _____ you from Italy?
  a Are   b Is
2 _____ Lisa. I'm Marisa.
  a Am not   b I'm not
3 Hi, Mark! _____ in my class.
  a You   b You're
4 A _____ from?
  B I'm from Russia.
  a Where are you   b Where you are
5 A Where's Gdansk?
  B _____ in Poland.
  a Is   b It's
6 A Is John married?
  B No, _____.
  a he isn't   b she isn't
7 A _____ English?
  B No, she's American.
  a She's   b Is she
8 They _____ Spanish. They're Mexican.
  a aren't   b not
9 A Are you on holiday?
  B No, _____ on business.
  a we're   b we
10 Ana and Julia are from Recife. _____ Brazilian.
  a She's   b They're
11 A _____ Mario and Renata Italian?
  B Yes, they're from Milan.
  a Are   b Is
12 A How old _____?
  B I'm 19.
  a you are   b are you
13 A _____ are you?
  B Fine, thanks. And you?
  a How   b Who
14 A _____ address?
  B It's 304 High Street.
  a What your   b What's your
15 A How _____ your surname?
  B G-A-R-C-I-A.
  a you spell   b do you spell

VOCABULARY

a Complete the chart.

Country	Nationality
China	Chinese
Turkey	1 _____
2 _____	Swiss
the United States	3 _____
4 _____	English
5 _____	Egyptian
Japan	6 _____

b Write the next number or word.

one, two, *three*
1 zero, one, _____
2 five, six, _____
3 eleven, twelve, _____
4 nineteen, twenty, _____
5 Tuesday, Wednesday, _____
6 Friday, Saturday, _____

c Complete the words.

Where are you **fr**_om_?
1 Good morning. O_____ your books, please. Page 19.
2 A S_____ I'm late.
  B OK. Sit d_____.
3 A What's the answer to number 10?
  B I don't **kn**_____.
4 A Excuse m_____, wh_____ *plato* in English?
  B Plate.
  A Can you r_____ that, please?
  B Yes. Plate.
5 A What's your phone n_____?
  B 029 2018 0583.
  A Thanks. What's your e_____?
  B It's tom@hotmail.com.

d Write the things in the classroom.

a dictionary

1 _____   2 _____   3 _____   4 _____

PRONUNCIATION

a Write the words for the sound pictures.

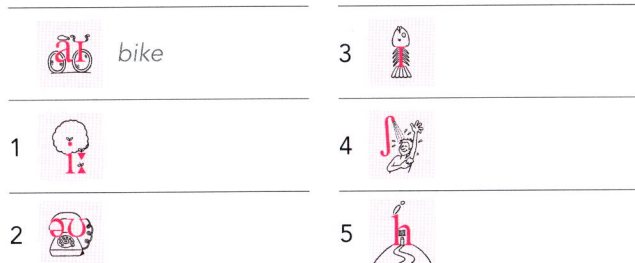

bike

1
2
3
4
5

b **p.134–5 Sound Bank** Look at more words with the sounds in **a**, and these sounds:

Practise saying the example words.

c Underline the stressed syllable.

<u>Sa</u>|tur|day
1 Chi|nese
2 fif|ty
3 fif|teen
4 to|mo|rrow
5 Ger|man

CAN YOU understand this text?

Read the profiles and complete the chart for Mark, Bianca, and Jacek. Then add information about you.

I'm **Mark Davis**. I'm from Seattle in the USA. I'm a teacher. I'm twenty-eight and I'm single.

I'm **Bianca Costa**. I'm from Rio in Brazil. I'm twenty. I'm single and I'm a student.

I'm **Jacek Popko**. I'm forty. I'm from Krakow in Poland. I'm married, with two children. I'm a doctor.

First name	Mark	Bianca	Jacek	_____ (= you)
Surname				
Age	28			
Nationality				
Marital status		single		
Occupation			doctor	

CAN YOU understand these people?

2.28 Watch or listen and answer the questions.

1 –   2 Vera   3 Richard   4 Mairi   5 Iain

1 The woman's name is ____.
   a Gayna
   b Jeina
   c Jayna
2 Vera is ____.
   a Mexican
   b Russian
   c Canadian
3 Richard is ____ years old.
   a 46
   b 56
   c 66
4 Mairi's phone number is ____.
   a 07564378
   b 07654378
   c 07563478
5 Iain's email address is ____.
   a iain.smith@yahoo.co.uk
   b iain.6@yahoo.com
   c iain.smith@yahoo.com

CAN YOU say this in English?

Tick (✓) the boxes.

Can you…?	Yes, I can.
1 say your name and where you are from	
2 ask where other people are from	
3 spell your name	
4 count from 0 to 100	
5 ask for and give personal information, e.g. name, address, age, etc.	
6 say your phone number	
7 use and understand classroom language	
8 check into a hotel	
9 book a table at a restaurant	

Go online to watch the video, review Files 1 & 2, and check your progress

3A Where are my keys?

Is it an ID card? — No, it's a credit card.

G singular and plural nouns, a / an **V** small things **P** /z/ and /s/, plural endings

1 VOCABULARY small things

a What are the four things? Can you remember?

b **V** p.119 **Vocabulary Bank** Small things

2 GRAMMAR singular and plural nouns, a / an

a Read the list. What do you think are the top four things?

Oh no! Where's my phone?

Every day people all over the world say, 'Oh no! Where's my...?' The top eight things that people look for are (not in the correct order):

- pens and pencils
- glasses and sunglasses
- keys (house keys and car keys)
- wallets and purses
- bank cards
- mobile phones
- umbrellas
- phone chargers

Adapted from the British Press

b ▶ 3.2 Listen and number the things 1–8 in the list in **a**. Is this order true for *you*?

> For me, number one is my glasses.

c Look at the photos. Complete the chart.

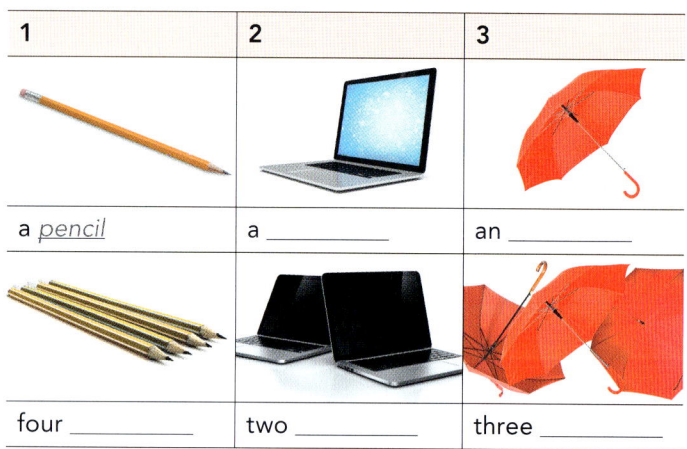

1	2	3
a *pencil*	a _____	an _____
four _____	two _____	three _____

d **G** p.96 Grammar Bank 3A

e **C** Communication Memory game p.81
Remember the things in the photo.

3 PRONUNCIATION /z/ and /s/, plural endings

a ▶ 3.5 Listen and repeat the words and sound.

z zebra	**z**ero Brazil is he's

b ▶ 3.6 Listen and repeat the plural words and sounds.

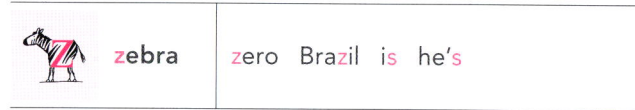

z	bag**s** phone**s** key**s** pen**s**

s	book**s** coat**s** passport**s** tablet**s**
/ɪz/	watch**es** glass**es** piec**es** purs**es**

c ▶ 3.7 Listen. Say the plural.

1 ◉ *It's a photo.* — They're photos.

4 LISTENING

a ◉ 3.8 Listen to five situations. Number the photos 1–5.

b Listen again. Write the small things for each situation.

1 _____
2 _____
3 _____
4 _____
5 _____

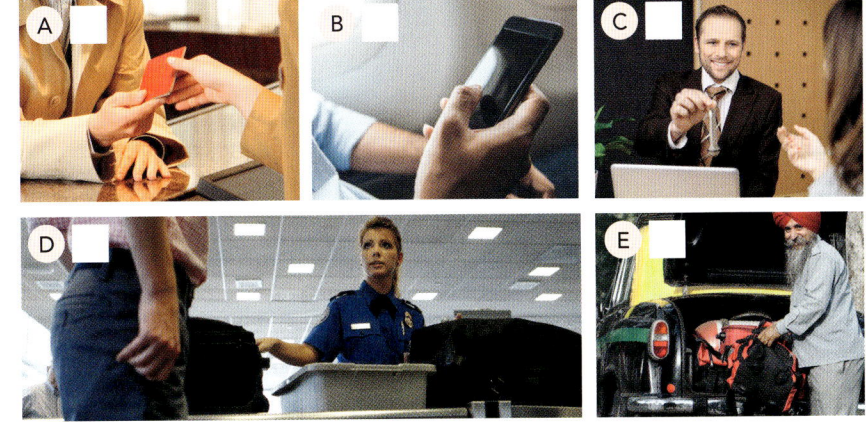

5 SPEAKING

a Look at the photos. What are the things? Work with a partner. **A** ask **B** about photo 1. **B** ask **A** about photo 2. Continue with the other photos.

What is it? — *(I think) it's a / an...*

What are they? — *(I think) they're...*

I don't know.

b What's in your bag or pocket? Tick (✓) the things.

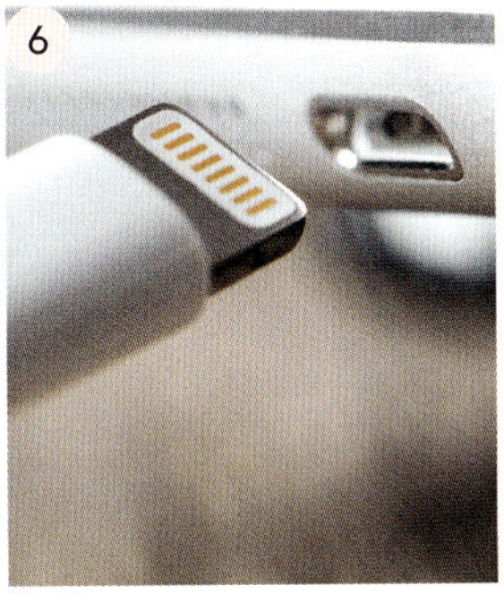

- a book
- a credit card
- glasses
- an ID card
- keys
- a pen
- a pencil
- a phone
- a photo
- a purse
- an umbrella
- a wallet

c Now tell a partner.

In my bag, I have a book, keys, a pen...

d What other things do you have in your bag or pocket? Ask your teacher.

What's...in English? How do you spell it?

WORDS AND PHRASES TO LEARN 3A

p.131 Listen and repeat the words and phrases.

Go online to review the lesson

3B Souvenirs

What are those? They're key rings.

G this / that / these / those **V** souvenirs **P** /ð/, sentence rhythm

1 VOCABULARY souvenirs

a ◆ 3.10 Look at the eight things. Listen and repeat the words.

1 a cap /kæp/   2 a football scarf /ˈfʊtbɔːl skɑːf/   3 a football shirt /ˈfʊtbɔːl ʃɜːt/   4 a key ring /ˈkiː rɪŋ/

5 a mug /mʌɡ/   6 a plate /pleɪt/   7 a teddy /ˈtedi/   8 a T-shirt /ˈtiː ʃɜːt/

b Cover the words and photos and look at the souvenir stall. Say the souvenirs 1–8.

c What are typical souvenirs in your country?

2 LISTENING

a ◆)) 3.11 Listen and complete the conversation with numbers.

Woman Excuse me. What are those?
Man They're T-shirts.
Woman How much are they?
Man They're ¹ £_____.

Woman And how much are these key rings?
Man They're ² £_____.
Woman And this mug?
Man ³ £_____.

Woman Is that a Manchester United shirt?
Man No, it's Arsenal.
Woman How much is it?
Man ⁴ £_____.
Woman Oh…no. Thank you. Bye.

b ◆)) 3.12 Listen and repeat the conversation in a. Then practise with a partner.

c ◆)) 3.13 Listen. What does the woman buy?

3 GRAMMAR this / that / these / those

a Read the conversation in **2** again. Complete the chart with the highlighted words.

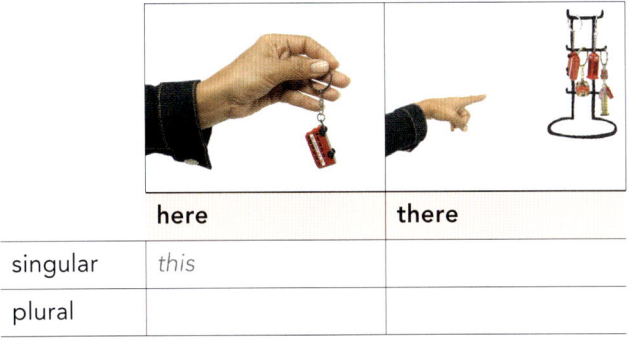

	here	there
singular	this	
plural		

b **G** p.96 Grammar Bank 3B

4 PRONUNCIATION & SPEAKING
/ð/, sentence rhythm

a ◆)) 3.15 Listen and repeat the words and sound.

| mother | this | that | these | those | the | they |

b ◆)) 3.16 Listen and complete the conversations with words and numbers.

1 How much is this _____?
   It's £_____.
2 How much is that _____?
   It's £_____.
3 How much are these _____?
   They're £_____.
4 How much are those _____?
   They're £_____.
5 Two _____, please.
   That's £_____.

c Listen again. Then repeat the conversations. Copy the rhythm.

d **C** Communication How much are these watches?
A p.79 B p.83 Role-play conversations.

WORDS AND PHRASES TO LEARN 3B

p.131 Listen and repeat the words and phrases.

Go online to review the lesson

2 Practical English Can I have an orang

understanding prices, buying lunch   **P** /ʊə/, /s/, and /k/

1 UNDERSTANDING PRICES

a ◉ 3.18 Listen and repeat.

ten pounds   fifty pence (fifty p)
ten euros   fifty cents
ten dollars   twenty-five cents

b Match the prices and words.

1	H	£12.75	A thirteen dollars twenty-five
2		€15.99	B eighty cents
3		$50.19	C five pounds thirty-five
4		£5.35	D fifteen euros ninety-nine
5		$13.25	E sixty pence
6		€3.20	F fifty dollars nineteen
7		€0.25	G three euros twenty
8		£1.50	H ~~twelve pounds seventy-five~~
9		60p	I one pound fifty
10		$0.80	J twenty-five cents

c ◉ 3.19 Listen and check. Then listen and repeat.

d Cover the words and look at the prices. Practise saying them.

e ◉ 3.20 Listen to four conversations. How much is it? Circle the correct price.

1	newspaper:	$2.50	$2.15
2	umbrella:	€15	€50
3	memory card:	$4.99	$9.49
4	train ticket:	£13.20	£30.20

2 PRONUNCIATION /ʊə/, /s/, and /k/

◉ 3.21 Listen and repeat the words and sounds.

🚶	t**ou**rist	**eu**ro **Eu**rope **Eu**ropean
🐍	**s**nake	**c**ent **c**ity pen**ce** pri**ce**
🗝	**k**ey	**c**offee **c**amera **c**redit **c**ard

> 🔍 **The letter c**
> c = /s/ before e and i, e.g. cent, city.
> c = /k/ before other letters, e.g. coffee.

3 ▶ BUYING LUNCH

a ◉ 3.22 Read the menu. Then listen and repeat the food, drinks, and prices.

b Practise with a partner. Ask the prices on the menu.

How much is a tuna sandwich?   £4.15.

uice, please?

c　🔊 3.23　Watch or listen to Rob in a London pub. Tick (✓) the things he orders on the menu in **a**.

d　Watch or listen again and complete the conversation.

Barman	Who's next?
Rob	Can I have a ¹_____ sandwich, please?
Barman	Anything else?
Rob	And a ²_____, please.
Barman	Ice and lemon?
Rob	³_____, thanks.
Barman	There you go.
Rob	Thanks. How much is it?
Barman	⁴_____.
Rob	Here you ⁵_____.
Barman	Thanks. Here's your change.

e　🔊 3.24　Watch or listen and repeat. Then practise the conversation with a partner.

f　Now role-play the conversation in pairs. **A** You are the barman. **B** Order food and a drink. Then change roles.

g　🔊 3.25　Watch or listen to Jenny and her friend Amy in a New York deli. How much is Jenny's lunch?

h　Watch or listen again. What do they have? Complete the chart.

Jenny	
Amy	

4　▶ USEFUL PHRASES

🔊 3.26　Watch or listen and repeat the useful phrases.

Can I have a cheese sandwich, please?	Here you are.
Anything else?	Here's your change.
And a Coke, please.	I'm fine, too.
Ice and lemon?	Wait for me.
No, thanks.	Sure!
How much is it?	Great idea.

Go online to watch the video and review the lesson

4A Meet the family

> Who's Selma?
> She's my boyfriend's sister.

G possessive adjectives, possessive 's   V people and family   P /ʌ/, /æ/, and /ə/

1 VOCABULARY people and family

a Look at the photos. Match the words to people 1–4.

☐ a boy   ☐ a girl   ☐ a man   ☐ a woman

b ▶ 4.1 Listen and check.

c V p.120 **Vocabulary Bank** People and family

2 PRONUNCIATION /ʌ/, /æ/, and /ə/

a ▶ 4.5 Listen and repeat the words and sounds.

⋀ up	husband Sunday son mother brother
🐱 cat	man family bag thanks that
🖥 computer	mother sister daughter children woman

> 🔍 /ə/
> /ə/ is a very common vowel sound in syllables that <u>aren't</u> stressed, e.g. final -er = /ə/ (moth<u>er</u>, daught<u>er</u>, etc.).

b ▶ 4.6 Listen and repeat. Practise the sentences.

'Is Justin your husband?' 'No, he's my brother.'
I have a big family. That's my grandfather.
The woman over there is my sister.

3 GRAMMAR possessive adjectives, possessive 's

a ▶ 4.7 Read and listen to the conversation on p.25. Do you think Sarah is a) a friend of the family b) a new babysitter?

b Look at photo A. Point to the people and say their names.

> He's Mark.

c Read and listen again. Then complete the chart with a highlighted phrase.

I	my husband
you	
he	
she	
it	
we	our children
you (plural)	
they	

d Read Part B again. Complete the sentences.
1 The name of the restaurant is _____ Bistro.
2 My _____ phone number is there, too.

e ▶ 4.8 Listen. Do you think Sarah is a good babysitter?

f G p.98 **Grammar Bank** 4A

g Point to people in the classroom. What are their names?

> What's his name?
> What's her name?

h Look at photo A on p.25. With a partner, say as much as you can about each person.

> His name's Oliver. He's Maria's son / Emma's brother.

Maria	Hi, Sarah! Come in.
Sarah	Thanks.
Maria	This is my husband, Mark.
Mark	Hello.
Sarah	Hi.
Maria	And these are our children.
Children	Hello!
Sarah	What are their names?
Maria	Her name's Emma, and his name's Oliver.
Emma	And this is our cat.
Sarah	Ah! What's its name?
Emma	Her name is Princess. She's a girl.
Sarah	Oh, sorry.

Maria	The name of the restaurant is Mario's Bistro. The phone number's on the table over there.
Sarah	Great, thanks.
Maria	And my husband's phone number is there, too.
Sarah	OK. And your number is in my phone.
Maria	Now, children. Sarah is your babysitter. Be good.
Children	OK, Mum.

4 LISTENING

a 4.11 Jane is in Italy with her friend Marina. It's her birthday. Look at her birthday card and listen. Who are the people?

1. Paul is _Jane_'s _brother_.
2. Hayley is _____'s _____.
3. Susan is _____'s _____.
4. Nicole is _____'s _____.
5. John is _____'s _____.

b Listen again. Answer the questions.
1. How old are Paul and Nicole?
2. Who are Sally and Max?

5 SPEAKING & WRITING

a Work with a partner:
- **A** and **B** write the names of six people (your family or friends) on a piece of paper.
- **A** give your piece of paper to **B**. **B** give your piece of paper to **A**.
- **A** ask **B** about his / her people. **B** ask **A** about his / her people.

Who's Marco?   He's my sister's husband.

b p.86 Writing A post about a photo
Write about a photo of your family.

WORDS AND PHRASES TO LEARN 4A

p.131 Listen and repeat the words and phrases.

4B The perfect car

> Is it a good car?
> No, it isn't. It's small and very slow.

G adjectives | V colours and common adjectives | P /ɑː/ and /ɔː/, linking

1 LISTENING & VOCABULARY
colours and common adjectives

a Do the quiz with a partner. Match the logos to the cars. What nationality are they?

> 1 is a Jaguar. I think it's English. Or American.

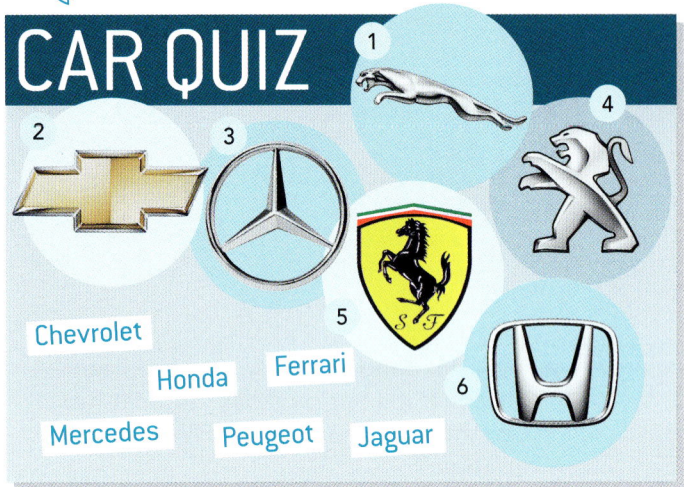

CAR QUIZ

Chevrolet · Honda · Ferrari · Mercedes · Peugeot · Jaguar

b 🔊 4.13 Listen and check.

c 🔊 4.14 Now look at the picture and listen to the conversation. Which car is perfect for the woman…?

   a in her opinion   b in her son's opinion

d Read the conversation. Write the highlighted words under the two cars.

Salesman	Is the car for you, sir?
Man	No, it's for my mother.
Woman	Yes, it's for me.
Salesman	For you, madam? Well, what about this blue car here? It's small and it's easy to park.
Man	Yes, Mum, it's perfect for you.
Woman	But it's very slow. And it's ugly.
Salesman	It's an electric car, madam. Very eco-friendly. They're good cars.
Woman	I prefer…this red car.
Man	But Mum, it's a sports car! It's very fast. And it's very expensive.
Woman	Yes, but it's my money. It's a beautiful car and I love it! How much is it?
Salesman	Come with me, madam.
Man	Mum! …

e 🔊 4.15 Listen and repeat the conversation. Then practise it in groups of three.

f V p.121 Vocabulary Bank Adjectives

g With a partner, talk about your car or your family's car.

> My car is a Peugeot 208. It's French. It's small and it's green. It isn't very fast.

2 GRAMMAR adjectives

a Circle a or b.
  1 a It's a beautiful car.
    b It's a car beautiful.
  2 a They're goods cars.
    b They're good cars.

b **G** p.98 **Grammar Bank 4B**

c ◉ 4.20 Listen and say the plural.

  1 ») an American car (American cars

3 PRONUNCIATION /ɑː/ and /ɔː/, linking

a ◉ 4.21 Listen and repeat the words and sounds.

car	f**a**st f**a**ther p**a**rk g**a**rden **a**re
horse	sh**or**t sp**or**t sm**a**ll **aw**ful

b ◉ 4.22 Listen. Practise the phrases.
  a big umbrella   an old man
  a short email   an orange coat
  brown eggs   an expensive watch

c ◉ 4.23 Listen and write five phrases.

d With a partner, look at the photos from **Vocabulary Bank** Adjectives and make sentences.

  (It's a black bag.   (They're blue keys.

4 SPEAKING

Talk in small groups.

I prefer small cities.) (*Me too.* (*I prefer big cities.*

big small
cities

Japanese Mexican
food

British American
films

cheap expensive
restaurants

old new
houses

long short
books

big small
dogs

black and white colour
photos

5 ▶ VIDEO LISTENING Beaulieu Motor Museum

a Watch the video *Beaulieu Motor Museum*. Which is your favourite car?

b Watch again. Mark the sentences **T** (true) or **F** (false).
  1 Beaulieu is a small village.
  2 It isn't famous.
  3 The National Motor Museum is 52 years old.
  4 The presenter's favourite car is the Bluebird.
  5 The Ferrari Dino is 14 years old.
  6 The Ford Anglia is an American car.
  7 It's famous because it's in the Star Wars films.
  8 The National Motor Museum has motorbikes, too.

c Do you think it's an interesting museum?

WORDS AND PHRASES TO LEARN 4B

p.131 Listen and repeat the words and phrases.

Go online to watch the video and review the lesson

3 & 4 Revise and Check

GRAMMAR

Circle a or b.

_____ 's your name?
a Who b What

1 Look! It's _____ email from Melanie.
   a an b a
2 A Where are my sunglasses? B _____ in your bag.
   a It's b They're
3 These are Swiss _____.
   a watchs b watches
4 Kyoto and Osaka are two important _____ in Japan.
   a citys b cities
5 A What's _____?
   B It's a key ring.
   a this b these
6 How much are _____ T-shirts?
   a those b that
7 Look at _____ house over there. It's beautiful.
   a this b that
8 _____ my friend, Tom.
   a It is b This is
9 He's Swiss. _____ name is Ken.
   a His b Her
10 We're Mr and Mrs Brown. _____ son is in class 4.
   a Our b Their
11 Justin is _____ brother.
   a Sophies b Sophie's
12 My _____ is Amanda.
   a name's wife b wife's name
13 These chairs are _____.
   a very expensive b very expensives
14 A Ferrari is a _____.
   a car fast b fast car
15 They're _____.
   a good photos b goods photos

VOCABULARY

a Write a / an + the things.

   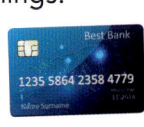   

a wallet   1 _____   2 _____

   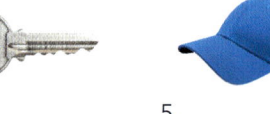

3 _____   4 _____   5 _____

b Complete the chart.

👨	man	father	2 _____	son	4 _____	boyfriend
👩	woman	1 _____	wife	3 _____	sister	5 _____

c Write the plural.

mother + father = _parents_
1 a woman two _____
2 a child three _____
3 a man four _____
4 a person 50 _____

d Write the colours.

☐ white
1 ■ _____   4 ■ _____
2 ■ _____   5 ■ _____
3 ■ _____   6 ■ _____

e Write the opposite adjectives.

fast _slow_
1 big _____   3 long _____
2 expensive _____ 4 new _____
                      5 ugly _____

PRONUNCIATION

a Write the words for the sound pictures.

_____   _____
🚲 bike   3 🖐
_____   _____
1 💻   4 🐕
_____   _____
2 ↑   5 🐈

b 📘 p.134–5 **Sound Bank** Look at more words with the sounds in **a**, and these sounds:

Practise saying the example words.

c Under<u>line</u> the stressed syllable.

   um|bre|lla   2 fa|mi|ly   4 ex|pen|sive
1 wo|man   3 o|range   5 sis|ter

28

CAN YOU understand this text?

a Read the two texts and write the people's names in the pictures.

My name's Jeremy Fisher and I'm from Liverpool, in the UK. I'm married to Anna and I have two children, a son and a daughter. My son's name is Matthew. He's 17. He's tall with dark hair. My daughter's name is Susanna. She's 19. I think my children are good-looking, probably because their mother is beautiful!

My name's Claire and I'm from Nantes in France. I'm 22. I have two sisters. Their names are Anne and Louise. Anne is 24. She's good-looking, with long blond hair. She isn't married. Louise is 31 and very different from Anne, but she's good-looking too. She's married. Her husband's name is Marius.

b Read again and answer the questions with a sentence.

1 What's Jeremy's surname?

2 Where is he from?

3 What's his son's name?

4 How old is Susanna?

5 What nationality is Claire?

6 Who is Anne?

7 Is she married?

8 How old is Louise?

CAN YOU understand these people?

4.25 Watch or listen and answer the questions.

1 Richard 2 Rachel 3 Kieran 4 Debra 5 Susan

1 What's in Richard's bag?
   a his keys
   b his coat
   c his camera
2 What's in Rachel's bag?
   a her phone, pencils and charger
   b her notebook, purse and passport
   c her phone, purse and umbrella
3 There are ____ people in Kieran's family.
   a 4
   b 5
   c 6
4 A cup of coffee in Debra's local coffee shop is ____.
   a cheap
   b £4
   c $4
5 Susan's car is ____.
   a big
   b green
   c a Fiat

CAN YOU say this in English?

Tick (✓) the boxes.

Can you…?	Yes, I can.
1 say what's in your bag	
2 talk about things with *this*, *that*, *these*, and *those*	
3 say who is in your family	
4 introduce somebody	
5 describe cars	
6 ask for things in a café or store	
7 ask about prices	

Go online to watch the video, review Files 3 & 4, and check your progress

5A A big breakfast?

> We have fruit and cereal for breakfast.

> I don't have breakfast. I have a coffee at work.

G present simple + and − : *I, you, we, they* **V** food and drink **P** /dʒ/ and /g/

1 VOCABULARY food and drink

a Re-order the letters to make food and drink words. Match them to photos A–E.

1 ☐ AET _____
2 ☐ ESHECE _____
3 ☐ GRANEO CUJIE _____ _____
4 ☐ WANDCHIS _____
5 ☐ GESG _____

b ◉ 5.1 Listen and check.

c **V** p.122 **Vocabulary Bank** Food and drink

2 READING & SPEAKING

a Look at the photos and read the article and comments. Who thinks breakfast is a) important, b) not important?

b ◉ 5.4 Complete the comments with food and drink words. Then listen and check.

c Read the comments again. (Circle) the places where they have breakfast. Underline the other words for food and drink.

d Is breakfast important for you? What do you have? Where do you have it?

A good breakfast – is it important?

Is breakfast a very important meal, or not important at all?
Scientists and doctors have different opinions: some think that a big breakfast is good for you, because you eat less during the day; others say that if you aren't hungry, don't have breakfast – it's only extra calories!

Is breakfast important for *you*? Send us a photo of your breakfast.

Comments

 Marta, Italy
I have breakfast in a great café near my office. I have a ¹**cr**oissant and coffee – an espresso with hot ²**m**_____. Mmmm. I love breakfast! It's my favourite meal.

 Paulo, Brazil
I have breakfast at home, but I don't have a big breakfast. I have ³**fr**_____ and ⁴**y**_____, and sometimes toast. It's a healthy breakfast. That's a good thing at the beginning of the day.

 Rob, UK
I don't eat in the morning – I'm not hungry. I just have a ⁵**c**_____ at work. But I have lunch early, at about 12.30.

 Sakura, Japan
I really like breakfast. It's an important meal for Japanese people. I have breakfast at home with my family. We have a traditional breakfast. It isn't very different from lunch and dinner. We have ⁶**r**_____, ⁷**f**_____, and miso soup and we drink green tea. We don't drink a lot of coffee in my family.

3 GRAMMAR present simple + and –: I, you, we, they

a Complete the sentences from the comments in **2**.

present simple + and –
+ **Marta**   1 I _____ breakfast in a great café.   **Sakura**   2 I really _____ breakfast.   3 We _____ a traditional breakfast.
– **Paulo**   4 I _____ _____ a big breakfast.   **Rob**   5 I _____ _____ in the morning.   **Sakura**   6 We _____ _____ a lot of coffee in my family.

b p.100 **Grammar Bank 5A**

c Look at **Vocabulary Bank** Food and drink **p.122** Say what you like 🙂 and don't like ☹.

I like fish. I don't like meat.

4 LISTENING

a 5.6 Listen to Anna talk about her favourite meal. Complete her column in the chart.

	Anna	Will	Sarah
Favourite meal	dinner	lunch	breakfast
Where?	¹At _____ or at a _____.	⁴At _____.	⁷Usually at _____. On Wednesdays at a _____.
Food	² _____ or _____ and _____.	⁵Different things but with _____.	⁸ _____ and an _____. On Wednesdays a _____.
Drink	³A glass of _____.	⁶ _____ and then a _____.	⁹ _____ or _____. On Wednesdays _____.

b 5.7 Now repeat for Will and Sarah.

c What's <u>your</u> favourite meal of the day?

5 PRONUNCIATION /dʒ/ and /g/

a 5.8 Listen and repeat the words and sounds.

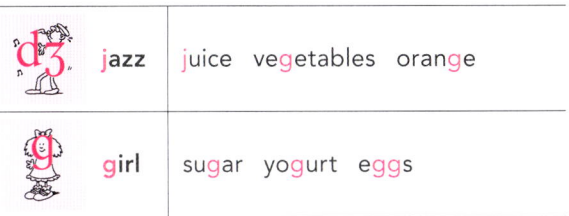

jazz	**j**uice ve**g**etables oran**g**e
girl	su**g**ar yo**g**urt e**gg**s

> 🔍 **g and j**
> Remember *j* always = /dʒ/. *g* is sometimes /g/ (e.g. su**g**ar) and sometimes /dʒ/ (e.g. oran**g**e), especially before *e*.

b 5.9 Listen. Practise the sentences.
I'm **J**ane. I like oran**g**e **j**uice and ve**g**etables.
I'm **G**race. I have e**gg**s, and coffee with su**g**ar.

6 SPEAKING

a Complete the sentences so they are true about <u>you</u> and people in your country.

Food: you and your country
You
I have breakfast _____. (Where?)
I have _____ for breakfast. (What?)
I have lunch _____. (Where?)
I have dinner with _____. (Who?)
I eat a lot of _____. (What?)
I love _____. (What?)
I don't like _____. (What?)
Your country
People have _____ for breakfast. (What?)
They have a big _____. (lunch / dinner)
They _____ a lot of food from other countries. (eat / don't eat)
They eat a lot of _____. (What?)
They drink a lot of _____. (What?)

b Talk to a partner. Say your first sentence. Then say *What about you?*

I have breakfast at home. What about you?
I have breakfast at home, too.

7 WRITING

 p.86 **Writing** A comment post Write about your breakfast.

WORDS AND PHRASES TO LEARN 5A

p.131 Listen and repeat the words and phrases.

 Go online to review the lesson **31**

5B A very long flight

> Do you live in New York?
>
> No, I don't. I live in London.

G present simple ?: I, you, we, they   **V** common verb phrases 1   **P** /w/ and /v/, sentence rhythm and linking

1 GRAMMAR present simple ?: I, you, we, they

a 🔊 5.11 Eve, a British woman, and Wendy, an American woman, are on a flight from London to New York. Listen to the conversation and number the pictures 1–4.

1	Eve	Do you like the ¹_____?
	Wendy	Yes, I do. It's very good.
	Eve	She's my favourite writer. I love her books.
2	Eve	Do you live in ²_____?
	Wendy	No, I don't. I live in London. My husband and I work for a British company.
	Eve	Oh! Do you have ³_____?
	Wendy	No, we don't.
	Eve	I have two sons and a daughter. David and Andrew are at university and Carla's at school. Look. Here are some photos… This is a photo of our holiday in Barbados. Do you know Barbados?
	Wendy	No, I don't.
3	Attendant	Do you want ⁴_____, fish, or pasta?
	Eve	Oh, fish, please.
	Wendy	Pasta for me, please.
	Eve	How's your pasta?
	Wendy	It's OK.
	Eve	This fish isn't very good. Excuse me, I don't like this fish. Can I have the ⁵_____, please?
	Attendant	I'm sorry, madam. It's finished.
4	Eve	Oh, I need to go to the toilet. Oops, sorry.
	Wendy	Excuse me. What ⁶_____ do we arrive?
	Attendant	In 25 minutes, madam.
	Wendy	That's good!

b Read the conversation and complete it with words from the list.

book   children   meat   New York   pasta   time

c Listen again and check.

d Underline the questions and short answers in parts 1 and 2 of the conversation.

e **G** p.100 Grammar Bank 5B

A

B

C

D

32

2 VOCABULARY common verb phrases 1

a Match the phrases.

1 I love — d — a in London.
2 I live — — b two sons and a daughter.
3 I work — — c for a British company.
4 I want — — d her books.
5 I have — — e the fish, please.

b **V** p.123 **Vocabulary Bank** Common verb phrases 1

c Write four true sentences about you, two positive and two negative.

I watch the BBC. I don't read a newspaper.

d In pairs, read your sentences to each other. Are any of them the same?

3 LISTENING

a ▶ 5.15 At the end of her holiday, Eve gets a taxi back to the airport. Read sentences 1–10 and look at the **bold** words. Then listen and (circle) a or b.

1 a Her flight is from **Newark** airport.
  b Her flight is from **JFK**.
2 a The traffic is **bad**.
  b The traffic is **good**.
3 a Eve is from **Manchester**.
  b Eve is from **London**.
4 a The taxi driver is from **New York**.
  b The taxi driver is from **Puerto Rico**.
5 a London is very **cheap**.
  b London is very **expensive**.
6 a The taxi driver has two **sons**.
  b The taxi driver has two **daughters**.
7 a The taxi is **$87.50**.
  b The taxi is **$87.15**.
8 a The taxi driver says 'Have a good **day**.'
  b The taxi driver says 'Have a good **flight**.'
9 a Eve **is late**.
  b Eve **isn't late**.
10 a The gate number is **B5**.
   b The gate number is **C5**.

b ▶ 5.16 Listen to what happens in the airport. Why does Eve say 'What a nice surprise!'?

4 PRONUNCIATION & SPEAKING
/w/ and /v/, sentence rhythm and linking

a ▶ 5.17 Listen and repeat the words and sounds.

witch	**w**ant **w**ork **w**hen **w**here
vase	**v**ery ha**v**e li**v**e TV

b ▶ 5.18 Listen. Notice the linked (‿) words.

1 A Do you **live** in a **flat**?
  B No, I **don't**. I **live** in a **house**.
2 A Do you **have** a big **family**?
  B Yes, I **do**. I **have** three **sisters**.
3 A Do you **watch** a lot of **TV**?
  B No, I **don't**. I **read books**.

c Listen again and repeat. Copy the rhythm.

d ▶ 5.19 Now listen and write five sentences.

e Complete 2–10 with a verb from the list.

drink eat go have listen live
need read speak watch

Do you...
1 *live* near here? / in a house or a flat?
2 _____ brothers and sisters? / a cat or a dog?
3 _____ TV on your phone? / YouTube videos?
4 _____ to pop music? / to classical music?
5 _____ a newspaper? / magazines?
6 _____ meat? / a lot of chocolate?
7 _____ Coke? / beer?
8 _____ French? / German?
9 _____ a new phone? / a new car?
10 _____ to a gym? / to the cinema at weekends?

f Ask and answer questions with a partner.

Do you live near here? *Yes, I do. I live very near.*
Do you live in a house or a flat? *I live in a small flat.*

WORDS AND PHRASES TO LEARN 5B

p.131 Listen and repeat the words and phrases.

EPISODE 3 Practical English What time is it?

telling the time   V the time, saying how you feel   P /ɒ/, silent consonants

1 ▶ TELLING THE TIME

a 🔊 5.21 Watch or listen and match the conversations to photos A–C.

1	Rob	I'm tired. What time is it?
	Alan	It's eleven o'clock.
	Rob	I need to go. I have a meeting in Oxford tomorrow morning.
	Alan	One more drink?
	Rob	Oh, OK!
2	Rob	Excuse me. What time is it?
	Woman	It's a quarter to eight. What time's your train?
	Rob	At seven forty-seven.
	Woman	You need to hurry! You only have two minutes.
	Rob	Thanks!
3	Rob	Hello. I'm Rob Walker. I'm sorry I'm late.
	Man	You're an hour late. It's half past ten.
	Rob	I know. I'm really sorry.

b 🔊 5.22 Watch or listen and repeat the conversations in **a**. Then practise them with a partner.

c Cover the conversations and look at the clocks in photos A–C. What time is it?

2 VOCABULARY the time

a 🔊 5.23 Listen and repeat the times.

It's three o'clock.   It's five past three.   It's ten past three.

It's (a) quarter past three.   It's twenty past three.   It's twenty-five past three.

It's half past three.   It's twenty-five to four.   It's twenty to four.

It's (a) quarter to four.   It's ten to four.   It's five to four.

b Cover the times. Look at the clocks and say the times.

c 🔊 5.24 Listen and draw the times on the clocks.

 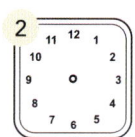 

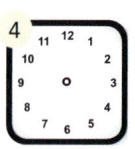  

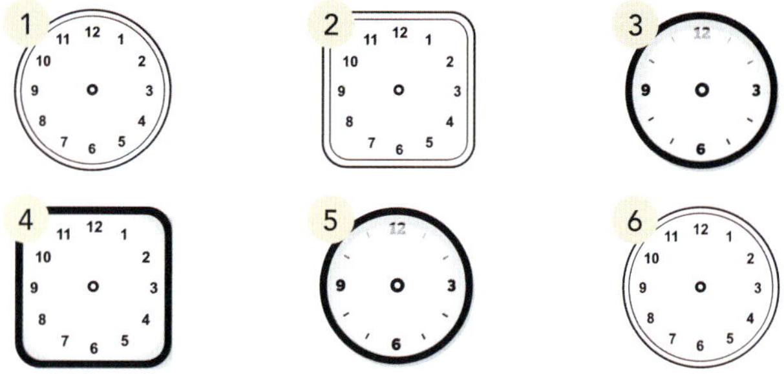

> **The time**
> 1 You can also say the time with numbers, e.g.
>   7.15 = (a) quarter past seven **OR** seven fifteen.
> 2 60 minutes /ˈmɪnɪts/ = one hour /aʊə/.

d Practise with a partner.

Number 1. What time is it?   *It's twenty to nine.*

e ⓒ **Communication** What time is it? **A** p.79 **B** p.83 Ask and answer about times.

3 PRONUNCIATION /ɒ/, silent consonants

a ◉ 5.25 Listen and repeat the words and sound.

 clock	wh**a**t **O**xford s**o**rry c**o**ffee

b ◉ 5.26 Listen and repeat the words. Practise saying them.

ei~~gh~~t   hal~~f~~   ~~h~~our   ~~k~~now   listen   ti~~r~~ed   t~~w~~o
We~~d~~nesday   w~~h~~at   ~~w~~rite

> 🔍 **Silent letters**
> Some English words have a 'silent letter', e.g. in *where*, you don't pronounce the *h* /weə/.

c ◉ 5.27 Listen to the conversations. Then practise with a partner.

A What time is it?
B It's half past two.

A Is the meeting on Wednesday?
B I don't know.

A Listen and write five sentences.
B Oh no! I'm tired.

4 VOCABULARY saying how you feel

a ◉ 5.28 Listen and repeat the sentences.

1 I'm tired.    2 I'm cold.    3 I'm <u>h</u>ungry.

4 I'm hot.   5 I'm <u>th</u>irsty.

b Match the sentences in **a** to a–e.

a ☐ Time for lunch.
b ☐ Time for bed.
c ☐ It's 5° (degrees /dɪˈɡriːz/) this morning.
d ☐ I need a glass of water.
e ☐ It's 35°!

c ◉ 5.29 Listen and check. How do <u>you</u> feel at the moment?

5 ▶ A NIGHT OUT

a ◉ 5.30 Watch or listen to Jenny and Amy. Tick (✓) the two places they go to.

☐ a bar
☐ a café
☐ a theatre
☐ a cinema
☐ a restaurant

b Watch or listen again. Complete sentences 1–3 with times.

1 The show is at _____.
2 Jenny and Amy meet at _____.
3 The show ends at _____.

6 ▶ USEFUL PHRASES

◉ 5.31 Watch or listen and repeat the useful phrases.

I need to go.	What a great show!
You need to hurry.	It's late and I'm tired.
You're an hour late.	Come on.
I'm really sorry.	OK. Let's go.
Don't worry.	

Go online to watch the video and review the lesson

6A A school reunion

G present simple: *he, she, it* V jobs and places of work P third person *-es*, sentence rhythm

> What does she do?
> She's a journalist. She works for a newspaper.

1 VOCABULARY jobs and places of work

a Look at the photos. What are their jobs?

1 He's a t_____ dr_____.
2 She's a t_____.
3 He's a r_____.

b p.124 **Vocabulary Bank** Jobs and places of work

c Choose a job from **Vocabulary Bank** Jobs and places of work. Ask five other students the questions. Answer their questions.

(What do you do?) (Where do you work?)

2 GRAMMAR present simple: *he, she, it*

a Look at the picture. Why are the people together?

b 6.4 Cover the conversation and listen. Mark the sentences **T** (true) or **F** (false).
   1 Anna is a journalist.
   2 She works for a magazine.
   3 Matt is a teacher.
   4 He teaches English.
   5 Laura is Matt's daughter.

c Listen again and read the conversation. Check your answers.

d Read the conversation again and complete the chart.

present simple, third person	
I / you	**he / she**
➕ **I work** for a newspaper.	**She** _____ for a newspaper.
➖ **I don't wear** glasses.	**She** _____ glasses.
❓ What **do you** do?	What _____ **he** do?

e p.102 **Grammar Bank 6A**

Julia   Who's that over there?
Sarah   It's Anna, you know, the intelligent girl.
Julia   She's very different! Her hair's blonde.
Sarah   Yes, and she doesn't wear glasses now.
Julia   What does she do?
Sarah   She's a journalist. She works for a newspaper – *The Times*, I think.
Julia   Is she good?
Sarah   I don't know. I don't read *The Times*.

Julia   And who's that man with grey hair? Is it Matt?
Sarah   Yes!
Julia   What does he do?
Sarah   He's a teacher. He teaches French.
Julia   Where does he work?
Sarah   At our old school!
Julia   No! At our old school?
Sarah   Yes, and he's married to Laura!
Julia   Laura? From our class? How awful! Is she here?
Sarah   Yes, she's with Matt.
Julia   Very ugly shoes.
Sarah   Yes, horrible.

Laura   Sarah, Julia, hi! Great to see you!
Julia   Hi, Laura. Wow, I *love* your shoes – they're beautiful…

3 PRONUNCIATION third person -es

a ▶ 6.6 Listen and (circle) the words where final -es = /ɪz/.

does   finishes   goes   likes   lives   teaches   watches   writes

b ▶ 6.7 Listen. Change the sentences. Use the third person.

1)) *I live in New York. He…*   (*He lives in New York.*

4 READING

a In what jobs in your country do people need to speak English?

b Read the article. Complete 1 and 2 with a job from **Vocabulary Bank** Jobs and places of work **p.124**.

Do you speak **English** at work?

What do these people have in common? A banker in Mexico City, a barman in a five-star hotel in Moscow, and a worker in the Hitachi electronics factory in Tokyo. They all speak English at work. Do you speak English at work? **Write and tell us.**

1 **Antonio** I work in a restaurant in Madrid. I'm a _____. I speak English at work every day, because a lot of tourists come here. I help customers with the menu and I say what the special dishes are. They are very happy because they can talk to me in English. A lot of tourists don't speak Spanish, but they usually speak English.

2 **Charlotte** I'm a _____ and I work in an office in Paris. It's a multinational company. When people from other countries visit the company, I need to welcome them in English. I also need to answer the phone in English. When we have meetings, we all speak in English, because it's the language of the company.

c ▶ 6.8 Now read again and listen. Check your answers.

d Answer the questions with a partner.
1 Why does Antonio speak English at work?
2 How does he help people?
3 Who does Charlotte work for?
4 What two things does she do in English?
5 Why do they speak English in meetings in her company?

> 🔍 **Why…? Because…**
> We use *Why…?* /waɪ/ to ask for a reason, and *Because…* /bɪˈkɒz/ to give a reason.
> ***Why** are the tourists happy?* ***Because** they can talk to Antonio in English.*

5 PRONUNCIATION & SPEAKING sentence rhythm

a ▶ 6.9 Listen to the conversation.

A **What** does he **do**?
B He's a **nurse**.
A **Where** does he **work**?
B He **works** in a **hospital**.
A Does he **speak English** at **work**?
B **No**, he **doesn't**.
A Does he **like** his **job**?
B **Yes**, he **does**.

b ▶ 6.10 Listen again and repeat. Copy the rhythm.

c Think of two people you know who have jobs. Ask and answer with a partner.
What / he (she) do?
Where / he (she) work?
/ he (she) speak English at work?
/ he (she) like his (her) job? Why?

Person number one is my mother.
(*What does she do?*

6 WRITING

Write paragraphs about the two people in **5c**.

My mother is a teacher. She works at a primary school in São Paulo. She doesn't speak English at work. She loves her job because she likes children!

WORDS AND PHRASES TO LEARN 6A

p.131 Listen and repeat the words and phrases.

6B Good morning, goodnight

What time do you usually get up?
I get up at 7.00.

G adverbs of frequency **V** a typical day **P** /j/ and /juː/, sentence rhythm

1 LISTENING & SPEAKING

a Read the questions in **Are you a morning person?** and think about your answers.

b ▶ 6.12 Look at the photos and listen to Hannah answer the questions in **a**. Does she like mornings?

Hannah works for the BBC. Her son, Kit, is three years old.

avocado

bath

c Listen again and write her answers to questions 1–8.

d ▶ 6.13 Listen and repeat questions 1–8.

e Ask your partner the questions. Is he or she a 'morning person'? Why (not)?

2 VOCABULARY a typical day

a **V** p.125 **Vocabulary Bank** A typical day

b Can you remember? Mime or draw five verb phrases for your partner to guess.

Are you a *morning* person?

1. What time do you usually get up?
2. Do you usually feel tired?
3. Do you have a shower or a bath in the morning?
4. Do you always have breakfast? Where?
5. What do you have for breakfast?
6. What time do you go to work (school / university)?
7. Do you usually need to hurry in the morning?
8. Do you like mornings? Why (not)?

3 GRAMMAR adverbs of frequency

a Match sentences 1–4 to a–d.

	M	Tu	W	Th	F
1 I **always** get up at 8.00, … c	✓	✓	✓	✓	✓
2 I **never** drink coffee, …	✗	✗	✗	✗	✗
3 I **usually** finish work at 6.00, …	✓	✓	✓	✓	✗
4 I **sometimes** watch TV, …	✗	✓	✗	✗	✓

a but on Fridays I finish at 3.00.
b or I read and listen to music.
c because I start work at 9.00.
d because I don't like it.

b **G** p.102 **Grammar Bank** 6B

4 PRONUNCIATION /j/ and /juː/, sentence rhythm

a ▶ 6.17 Listen and repeat the words and sounds.

yacht	yes you young yellow
/juː/	usually student music beautiful

b ▶ 6.18 Listen and repeat. Copy the rhythm.

What time do you **usually have lunch**?
At **half past one**.
What time do you **usually have dinner**?
At about **eight o'clock**.
What time do you **usually go** to **bed**?
At **half past eleven**.

c Ask and answer the questions with a partner.

d In pairs, make true sentences about you. Use *always, usually, sometimes,* or *never*.

- listen to the radio in the car
- read a newspaper in the morning
- speak English outside class
- watch TV in the evening
- have a big lunch
- do housework at the weekend
- eat fast food
- drink espresso

I always listen to the radio in the car. I listen to Radio 2.

5 SPEAKING & WRITING

a Use the pictures in **Vocabulary Bank A typical day p.125** to tell your partner about your typical evening. Use adverbs of frequency.

I never make dinner. My father makes it. We usually have dinner at half past eight.

b Write about **your** typical morning and afternoon. Use adverbs of frequency (*always, usually,* etc.) and time words (*then, after breakfast,* etc.).

6 ▶ VIDEO LISTENING A day in the life of a New York tour guide

a Look at photos A–F from the video *A day in the life of a New York tour guide*. With a partner, number the photos 1–6.

b Watch the video and check your order.

Glossary

US English	British English
an apartment	a flat
the subway	the Underground

c Watch again. Mark the sentences **T** (true) or **F** (false).
1 Peter lives in an apartment in Brooklyn.
2 He gets up at seven o'clock.
3 He usually has an omelette for breakfast.
4 He works for a company called Real World Tours.
5 His tours begin at eleven o'clock.
6 He usually has a sandwich for lunch.
7 The tour ends in Wall Street.
8 Peter goes home by subway.
9 In the evening he reads or watches TV.
10 Every day he walks about ten miles.

d Watch some extracts from the video. Complete the sentences with a 'time' word or phrase.
1 _____ _____ he goes there by subway.
2 _____ work, Peter takes the subway back to Brooklyn.
3 _____ he relaxes.

e Do you think Peter's job is easy or difficult? Why?

WORDS AND PHRASES TO LEARN 6B

p.131 Listen and repeat the words and phrases.

Go online to watch the video and review the lesson

5 & 6 Revise and Check

GRAMMAR

Circle a or b.

_____ 's your name?
a Who   b What

1 In Japan, we _____ rice for breakfast.
  a have   b has
2 They _____ meat.
  a don't eat   b not eat
3 You _____ a lot of fast food. It isn't good for you.
  a eats   b eat
4 I _____ tea, I prefer coffee.
  a don't drink   b 'm not drink
5 _____ you want a Coke?
  a Are   b Do
6 A Do they live near here?
  B Yes, they _____.
  a do   b live
7 _____ Mexican food?
  a Like you   b Do you like
8 A What time _____?
  B At 5.30.
  a do we arrive   b we arrive
9 _____ she speak Spanish?
  a Do   b Does
10 He _____ for a fashion magazine.
  a works   b work
11 My brother _____ children.
  a don't have   b doesn't have
12 She _____ to the gym after work.
  a gos   b goes
13 He _____ a shower before breakfast.
  a always has   b has always
14 I _____ to bed before 12.00.
  a don't never go   b never go
15 What time _____ lunch?
  a you have usually   b do you usually have

VOCABULARY

a Write the words.

bread   1 _____   2 _____
3 _____   4 _____   5 _____

b Complete the verbs.

h_ave_ a shower
1 r_____ the newspaper   6 w_____ TV
2 l_____ to the radio   7 d_____ housework
3 g_____ shopping   8 sp_____ English
4 l_____ in a flat   9 h_____ two children
5 g_____ up in the morning   10 dr_____ tea

c Complete the words.

My wife's a t_eacher_ in a school in the city.
1 I don't have a job. I'm u_____.
2 He's a w_____. He works in a restaurant.
3 My grandfather doesn't work now. He's r_____.
4 My sister's a n_____. She works in a big hospital.
5 He's a j_____. He writes for the New York Times.

d Write the times.

(a) quarter past ten   1 _____   2 _____
3 _____   4 _____   5 _____

PRONUNCIATION

a Write the words for the sound pictures.

- bike
- 3 ___
- 1 ___
- 4 ___
- 2 ___
- 5 ___

b **p.134–5 Sound Bank** Look at more words with the sounds in **a**, and these sounds:

Practise saying the example words.

c Underline the stressed syllable.

break|fast   2 po|lice|man   4 u|sual|ly
1 po|ta|toes   3 al|ways   5 ce|re|al

CAN YOU understand this text?

a Read the text and complete it with words from the list.

coffee   diet   don't   every   good   hamburgers   meat
potatoes   small   stop   vegetables

EAT THE JAPANESE WAY

Doctors say that the traditional _diet_ in Japan and other Asian countries is very healthy.

WHY IS IT GOOD FOR YOU?

In Japan, people don't eat a lot of red ¹_____, butter, or cheese. They eat a lot of rice and fish and fresh fruit and ²_____. This diet is very ³_____ for your heart and people in Japan live longer than in other countries.

HOW TO EAT LIKE THE JAPANESE

- Eat rice with your meals and don't eat a lot of ⁴_____, especially chips.
- Eat a lot of fish. ⁵_____ eat a lot of meat, for example steak and ⁶_____.
- Eat fresh fruit and vegetables ⁷_____ day.
- Drink green tea, not ⁸_____.
- Eat on ⁹_____ plates. Eat slowly. ¹⁰_____ eating when you are full.

b Do you eat 'the Japanese way'?

CAN YOU understand these people?

▶ 6.20 Watch or listen and answer the questions.

1 John   2 Hanna   3 Lisa   4 Susan   5 Kieran

1 For breakfast John usually has ____.
  a tea and cereal
  b tea and toast
  c coffee and toast
2 Hanna lives in ____.
  a a flat in London
  b a house near London
  c a house near Manchester
3 Lisa's son is ____.
  a 1
  b 6
  c 16
4 Susan ____.
  a doesn't work
  b is a taxi driver
  c works in an office
5 Kieran gets up at ____ at weekends.
  a 8 a.m.
  b 9 a.m.
  c 10 a.m.

CAN YOU say this in English?

Tick (✓) the boxes.

Can you…?	Yes, I can.
1 say what you do (your job or activity)	☐
2 ask what other people do	☐
3 say what you have for breakfast	☐
4 say what people eat in your country	☐
5 ask and say what time it is	☐
6 say what you do on a typical day	☐
7 ask about other people's days	☐

Go online to watch the video, review Files 5 & 6, and check your progress

Communication

1B WHERE IS IT? Student A

a   Ask **B** questions for your cities.

Where's Izmir?

1 **Izmir** is in Turkey.
2 **Atlanta** is in the United States.
3 **Basel** is in Switzerland.
4 **Curitiba** is in Brazil.
5 **Dortmund** is in Germany.
6 **Gdansk** is in Poland.
7 **Hong Kong** is in China.
8 **Luxor** is in Egypt.

b   Answer **B**'s questions with a country.

It's in…   *I think it's in…*   *I don't know.*   ← p.8

PE1 HIT THE SHIPS Student A

a   Draw five 'ships' in **Your ships**.

Your ships — grid A–J × 1–10

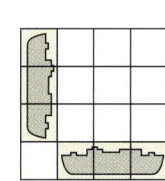

One ship = three squares

B's ships — grid A–J × 1–10

b   Try to 'hit' **B**'s ships. Say a square, e.g. H8. If **B** says *Hit*, tick (✓) the square in **B**'s ships. If **B** says *Nothing*, cross (✗) the square.

H8?   *Nothing.*   *B7?*   *Hit!*

c   **B** says a square. Say *Hit* or *Nothing*.   ← p.10

2A IS SUSHI CHINESE? Student A

1 _____ sushi Chinese?
2 _____ the Rolling Stones American?
3 _____ Giorgio Armani Italian?
4 _____ Victoria Beckham Australian?
5 _____ the pyramids Egyptian?

6 Gisele Bündchen is Brazilian.
7 Lada cars are Russian.
8 Tacos are Mexican.
9 Antonio Banderas is Spanish.
10 Swatch and Rolex are Swiss.

a   Ask **B** about 1–5. Use *Is…?* or *Are…?* Tick (✓) if the answer is yes. If the answer is no, write the nationality.

Is sushi Chinese?

b   Answer **B**'s question about 6–10.

No, he / she / it isn't. He / She / It's…
Yes, they are.
No, they aren't. They're…   ← p.13

2B PERSONAL INFORMATION Student A

a Interview **B** and complete **B**'s form.

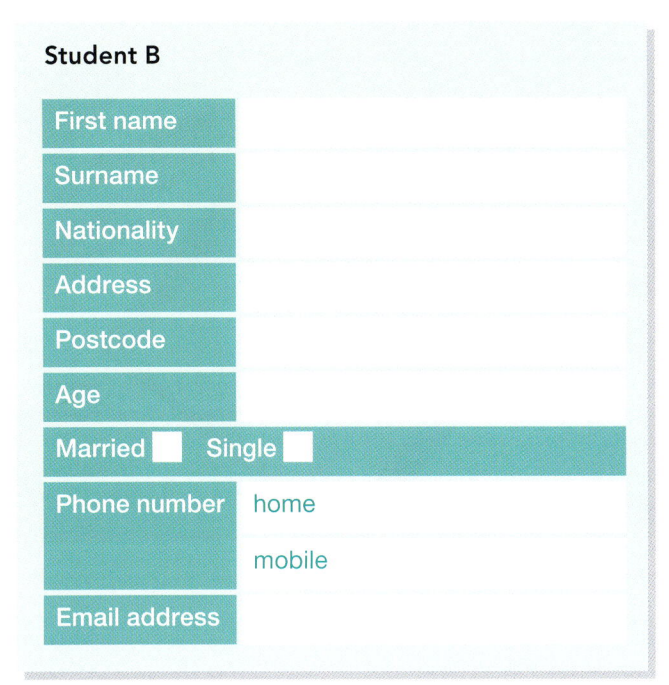

What's your first name? — *Chris.*
How do you spell it? — *C-H-R-I-S.*

Student B

First name	
Surname	
Nationality	
Address	
Postcode	
Age	
Married ☐ Single ☐	
Phone number	home
	mobile
Email address	

b Answer **B**'s questions. Use the information in the **YOU** form.

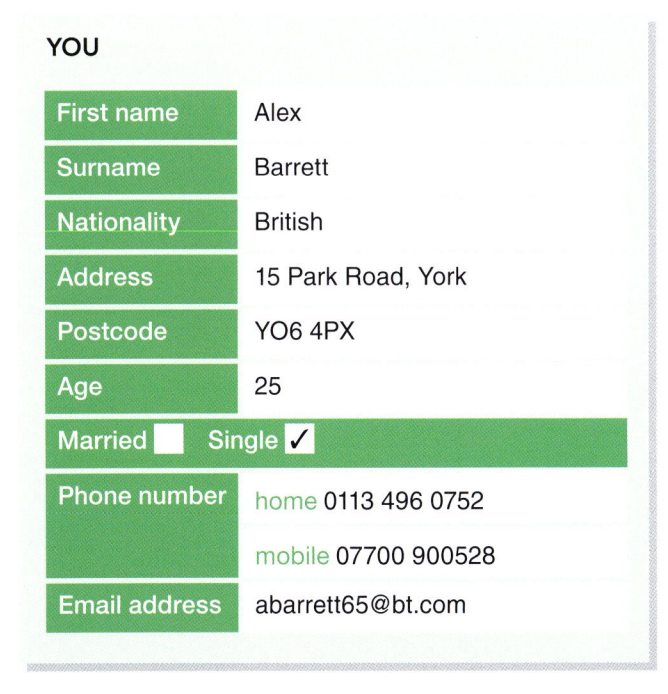

YOU

First name	Alex
Surname	Barrett
Nationality	British
Address	15 Park Road, York
Postcode	YO6 4PX
Age	25
Married ☐ Single ✓	
Phone number	home 0113 496 0752
	mobile 07700 900528
Email address	abarrett65@bt.com

← p.15

3B HOW MUCH ARE THESE WATCHES? Student A

a Look at your picture. You are a customer. Ask **B** about the missing prices. Use *this / that* for singular objects **OR** *these / those* for plural objects. Write the prices.

How much is this mug? — *It's…*

b Now **B** is a customer. Answer **B**'s questions with a price.

It's / They're…pounds.

← p.21

PE3 WHAT TIME IS IT? Student A

a Ask **B** a question to complete the time on clock 1.

Clock 1: What time is it?

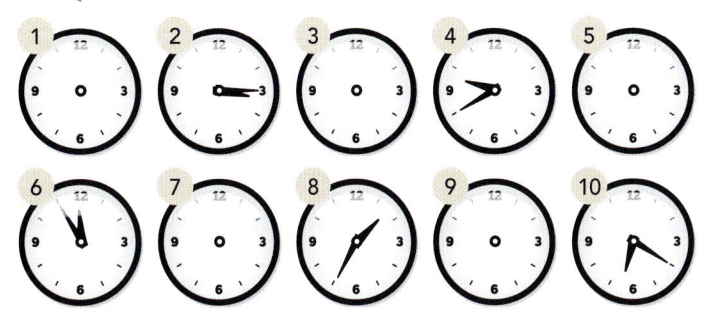

b Answer **B**'s question about clock 2.

It's…

c Continue with the other clocks. ← p.34

3A MEMORY GAME Students A+B

a   Look at the photo for 30 seconds.

b   Close your book. In pairs, can you remember all the things?

A watch.   *No, two watches, I think.*   ⟲ p.18

1B WHERE IS IT? Student B

a Answer **A**'s questions with a country.

(*It's in…* (*I think it's in…* (*I don't know.*

b Ask **A** questions for your cities.

(*Where's Acapulco?*

1 **Acapulco** is in Mexico.
2 **Las Vegas** is in the United States.
3 **Manchester** is in England.
4 **Milan** is in Italy
5 **Osaka** is in Japan.
6 **Rostov** is in Russia.
7 **Toulouse** is in France.
8 **Valencia** is in Spain.

← p.8

PE1 HIT THE SHIPS Student B

a Draw five 'ships' in **Your ships**.

Your ships

	1	2	3	4	5	6	7	8	9	10
A										
B										
C										
D										
E										
F										
G										
H										
I										
J										

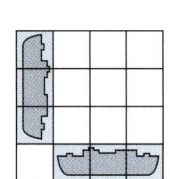

One ship = three squares

A's ships

	1	2	3	4	5	6	7	8	9	10
A										
B										
C										
D										
E										
F										
G										
H										
I										
J										

b **A** says a square, e.g. *H8*. If you have a ship in H8, say *Hit*. If not, say *Nothing*.

H8?) (*Nothing.*   *B7?*) (*Hit!*

c Try to 'hit' **A**'s ships. Say a square, e.g. *B3*. If **A** says *Hit*, tick (✓) the square in **A**'s ships. If **A** says *Nothing*, cross (✗) the square.

← p.10

2A IS SUSHI CHINESE? Student B

1 Sushi is Japanese.
2 The Rolling Stones are British.
3 Giorgio Armani is Italian.
4 Victoria Beckham is British.
5 The Pyramids are Egyptian. 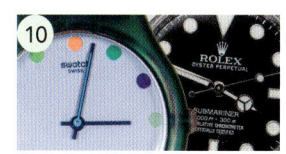
6 _____ Gisele Bündchen German?
7 _____ Lada cars Polish?
8 _____ tacos Mexican?
9 _____ Antonio Banderas Italian?
10 _____ Swatch and Rolex Swiss?

a Answer **A**'s question about 1–5.

Yes, he / she / it is.
No, he / she / it isn't. He / She / It's…
Yes, they are.
No, they aren't. They're…

b Ask **A** about 6–10. Use *Is…?* or *Are…?* Tick (✓) if the answer is yes. If the answer is no, write the nationality.

(*Is Gisele Bündchen German?*

← p.13

2B PERSONAL INFORMATION Student B

a Answer **A**'s questions. Use the information in the **YOU** form.

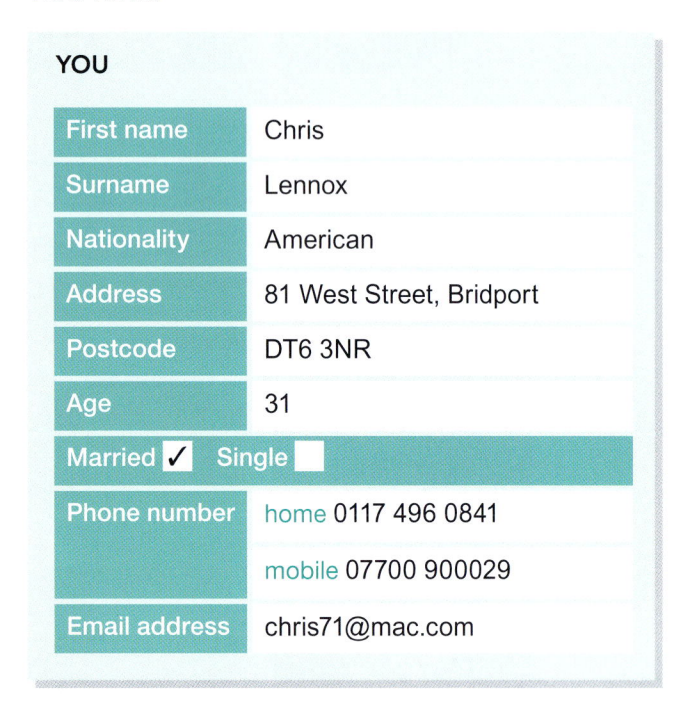

YOU	
First name	Chris
Surname	Lennox
Nationality	American
Address	81 West Street, Bridport
Postcode	DT6 3NR
Age	31
Married ✓ Single ☐	
Phone number	home 0117 496 0841
	mobile 07700 900029
Email address	chris71@mac.com

b Interview **A** and complete **A**'s form.

What's your first name? *Chris.*
How do you spell it? *C-H-R-I-S.*

Student A	
First name	
Surname	
Nationality	
Address	
Postcode	
Age	
Married ☐ Single ☐	
Phone number	home
	mobile
Email address	

← p.15

3B HOW MUCH ARE THESE WATCHES? Student B

a Look at your picture. **A** is a customer. Answer **A**'s questions with a price.

It's / They're…pounds.

b Now you are a customer. Ask **A** about the missing prices. Use *this / these* OR *that / those*. Write the prices.

How much is this flag? *It's…*

← p.21

PE3 WHAT TIME IS IT? Student B

a Answer **A**'s question about clock 1.

It's…

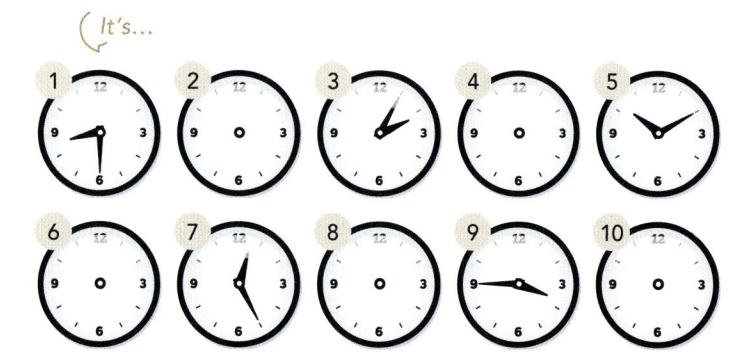

b Ask **A** a question to complete the time on clock 2.

Clock 2: What time is it?

c Continue with the other clocks.   ← p.34

Writing

1 A FORM

a Look at the form. Match each part to a question a–h below.

a ☐ Are you married?
b ☐ What's your home phone number?
c ☐ What's your postcode?
d ☐ How old are you?
e ☐ What's your email?
f ☐ 1 What's your name?
g ☐ What's your mobile number?
h ☐ What's your address?

CREDIT CARD Application form

1 First name

Surname

Title: Mr ☐ Ms ☐ Mrs ☐

2 Age

3 Married ☐ Single ☐
Divorced / Separated ☐

4 Address

5 Postcode

6 Email

Phone number 7 home

8 mobile

b Complete the form for you. Tick (✓) your title, too.

🔍 **Titles**
Mr = a man, Ms = a woman,
Mrs = a married woman

Capital letters
Adam Davis **NOT** adam davis
245 Green Street **NOT** 245 green street
London **NOT** london

← p.15

2 A POST ABOUT A PHOTO

a Read about Alice and her family. Write the numbers of the people on the photo.

My name is ¹Alice and I'**m** from Toulouse in France**.** This is a photo of my family. My father'**s** name is ²Henri**,** and my mother's name is ³Cécile. I have a sister, ⁴Pauline, and a brother, ⁵Olivier. We have a dog. His name is ⁶Toto. Do you like my photo**?**

b Look at the highlighted punctuation in the text and read the information box.

🔍 **Punctuation**
full stop (.)   My name is Alice and I'm from Toulouse.
                NOT My name is Alice and I'm from Toulouse
comma (,)   I have a sister, Pauline, and a brother, Olivier.
question mark (?) Do you like my photo?
apostrophe (') I'm from Toulouse. **NOT** Im from Toulouse.
                My father's name… **NOT** My fathers name…

c Post a photo of your family and write about it.   ← p.25

3 A COMMENT POST

a Read Marcos's comment. Do you like his breakfast?

LET'S CHAT! TODAY'S QUESTION:

Is breakfast important for you? What do you have? Where do you have it?

Marcos, Cuenca, Spain *7 mins ago*
Breakfast is very important for me! I have fruit, usually an orange **or** an apple.
Then I have bread with butter **and** jam, and a cup of coffee.
I usually have breakfast at home, **but** at the weekend I have it in a bar near my house. I think my breakfast is very healthy.

b Look at the highlighted words. Complete sentences 1–3 with *and*, *or*, or *but*.

1 I eat fish, _____ I don't eat meat.
2 Do you have tea _____ coffee for breakfast?
3 I have a brother _____ a sister.

c Write a comment about *your* breakfast. What do you have? Is it healthy? Use *and*, *but*, and *or* to connect.   ← p.31

Listening

🔊 **1.42**

Hello. I'm Rob. I'm from London. I'm a journalist. Today I'm in Poland. I'm not on holiday. I'm here for work.

🔊 **1.45**

Hi. I'm Jenny Zielinski. I'm from New York. Tomorrow's my birthday, and my favourite restaurant in New York is Locanda Verde. It's Italian.

🔊 **1.46**

Waiter Locanda Verde. Good morning. How can I help you?
Jenny Hello. A table for tomorrow, please.
Waiter Tomorrow…er, Tuesday?
Jenny Yes, that's right.
Waiter How many people?
Jenny Three.
Waiter What time?
Jenny Seven o'clock.
Waiter What's your name, please?
Jenny Jenny Zielinski. That's Z-I-E-L-I-N-S-K-I.
Waiter Thank you, Ms, er, Zielinski. OK. So, a table for three on Tuesday at seven.
Jenny Great. Thanks. Bye.
Waiter Goodbye, see you tomorrow.

🔊 **2.26**

1 **A** Great. OK, see you on Tuesday.
  B Yes. Oh, what's your phone number?
  A It's, er, 020 7946 0415.
2 **A** Thank you. What's your address, please?
  B It's 57 King Street. Very near here.
3 **A** Come in, sit down. You're Martin Blunt, right?
  B Yes.
  A And how old are you, Mr Blunt?
  B I'm 39…
4 **A** Thank you very much. Er, one more thing. What's your email?
  B It's james85@ukmail.com.

🔊 **3.2**

What are the top things people look for every day? At number 8, it's…wallets and purses.
At number 7, umbrellas.
At number 6, bank cards – credit cards or debit cards.
At number 5, phone chargers.
And now for the top four.
At number 4, glasses and sunglasses.
At number 3, pens and pencils.
And at number 2, mobile phones.
And at number 1, – yes, that's right – keys. House keys and car keys.
So, try to find a safe place…

🔊 **3.8**

1 Please take out your laptops… All laptops out of cases, please.
2 Please switch off all mobile phones and electronic devices.
3 **A** Excuse me, is this your bag?
  B Oh yes! Thanks very much!
4 **A** Hi. My name's Sam Smith. I have a reservation.
  B Can I see your passport, please?
  A Sure, here you are.
5 **A** OK, Ms Jones. You're in room 315. Here's your key.
  B Thank you very much. Er, where's the lift?

🔊 **3.13**

Man Excuse me, Miss. Is this your phone?
Woman Oh! Yes, it is. Thank you very much.
Man You're welcome. It's a very nice phone! The new iPhone.
Woman Sorry? Oh yes.
Man A souvenir for your family? A football shirt is only £25!
Woman OK. An Arsenal football shirt, please.
Man And a T-shirt?
Woman Yes, and a T-shirt!

🔊 **3.20**

1 **Man** *The New York Times*, please.
  Woman Here you are.
  Man How much is it?
  Woman It's two dollars fifty.
2 **Man** An umbrella, please.
  Woman For how much?
  Man Fifteen euros, please.
  Woman Here you are.
  Man Thanks.
3 **Man 1** A memory card, please.
  Man 2 Two gigs or four?
  Man 1 Two, please. How much is it?
  Man 2 Nine dollars forty-nine.
  Man 1 Is a credit card OK?
  Man 2 Sure.
4 **Woman** A one-way ticket to Oxford, please.
  Man Thirty pounds twenty p, please.
  Woman Here you are.
  Man Thank you.

🔊 **3.25**

Assistant Hi. How can I help you?
Jenny Hi. How much is this tuna salad?
Assistant It's seven twenty.
Jenny OK, fine. And this mineral water, please.
Assistant That's nine dollars seventy cents.
Jenny Here you are.
Assistant Thank you. Have a nice day.
Amy Jenny!
Jenny Amy! Hi, how are you?
Amy I'm fine. How are you?
Jenny I'm fine, too.
Amy What's that?
Jenny Oh, just a salad and some water.
Amy You are good! Look, wait for me. We can have lunch together in the park.
Jenny Sure! Great idea.
Amy Can I have a cheese sandwich, a cappuccino, and a brownie, please?

4.11

Marina What a lovely card!
Jane Yes, it's from my family.
M Can I see?
J Sure.
M Who's Paul? Is he your brother?
J Yes, he's my brother and Hayley's his girlfriend.
M How old is Paul?
J He's twenty-nine. No, he's thirty.
M What about Susan? Is she your sister?
J No, Susan's my brother Jerry's wife. And Sally's their daughter.
M Oh yes, I remember. The baby in the photo on your phone.
J Yes. She's so beautiful.
M So who's Nicole?
J She's my sister.
M Is John her husband?
J No, he's her boyfriend – they aren't married. Perhaps one day.
M And how old's Nicole?
J She's twenty-six.
M And who's Max?
J He's my dog!
M Ah. What kind of dog is he?

4.13

1 It's a Jaguar. It's English.
2 It's a Chevrolet. It's American.
3 It's a Mercedes. It's German.
4 It's a Peugeot. It's French.
5 It's a Ferrari. It's Italian.
6 It's a Honda. It's Japanese.

5.6

Anna My favourite meal of the day is dinner. I usually have dinner at home, but sometimes at a restaurant. I usually have meat or fish and vegetables, and if I'm at a restaurant, I have a glass of wine.

5.7

Will My favourite meal of the day is lunch. I'm always hungry then. I have lunch at work – we have a canteen there. I have different things for lunch but always with chips – I love chips. Sometimes a burger and chips, sometimes fish and chips. I drink water with my lunch but after lunch I have a coffee, an espresso.

Sarah My favourite meal of the day is breakfast. I usually have it at home, but on Wednesday I have my yoga class and I have breakfast at a café near the yoga studio. At home I have fruit and an egg, and coffee or tea. But at the café I have a croissant and hot chocolate.

5.15

Taxi driver Where to ma'am?
Eve Hello. To the airport, please.
Taxi driver JFK or Newark?
Eve JFK, please.
Eve Oh dear. The traffic is bad this morning.
Taxi driver Yes. It's terrible. Where are you from?
Eve I'm from Manchester but I live in London. Are you from New York?
Taxi driver No, ma'am, I'm from Puerto Rico.
Eve Oh, do you like New York?
Taxi driver It's a great city, but it's very expensive.
Eve London is very expensive, too. Do you have children?
Taxi driver I have two daughters.
Eve Oh really? I have two sons and a daughter. David and Andrew are at university, and Carla's at school…
Taxi driver OK. Here we are.
Eve How much is that?
Taxi driver That's $87.50.
Eve Oh. Here's $100. Keep the change.
Taxi driver Thanks. Have a good flight!
Eve I need to hurry. I'm late!
Announcement This is the final call for flight BA641 to London Heathrow. Would all passengers please proceed to gate B5?

5.30

Amy Hi. Sorry I'm late. What time's the show?
Jenny Don't worry. It's at eight o'clock.
Amy What time is it now?
Jenny It's OK. It's only twenty to eight.
Amy What a great show!
Jenny Yes, fantastic. I'm hungry. Do you want a pizza?
Amy What time is it?
Jenny Um, quarter to eleven.
Amy It's late and I'm tired.
Jenny Come on. I know a really good Italian restaurant near here.
Amy Oh, OK. Let's go.

6.12

I Hannah works for the BBC. She has a son, Kit, who's three years old.
I Hannah, what time do you usually get up?
H I get up at 7.00. But I also get up in the night, because Kit usually calls me. I tell him to sleep, but he usually comes into my bed.
I Do you usually feel tired?
H Yes, I always feel tired!
I Do you have a shower or a bath in the morning?
H I turn on the TV for Kit and then I have a bath in five minutes.
I Do you always have breakfast?
H Yes, I need breakfast every day!
I Where do you have it?
H I have it in a café on the way to work.
I What do you have for breakfast?
H I have a coffee and sometimes I have some toast with avocado. It's delicious.
I What time do you go to work?
H The perfect time to leave the house is at 8.00, but we usually leave at twenty past eight.
I Do you usually need to hurry in the morning?
H Yes, always!
I Do you like mornings?
H Yes. I love mornings.
I Why?
H Because I love my job, and I'm happy to go to work!

GRAMMAR BANK

1A verb *be* (singular): *I* and *you*

🔊 **1.4** Listen and repeat the examples. Then read the rules.

Full form	Contraction
+ I **am** Helen.	**I'm** Helen.
You are Tom.	**You're** Tom.
− I **am not** Ellen.	**I'm not** Ellen.
You are not Dom.	**You aren't** Dom.

- *I'm* Helen.   **NOT**   ~~i'm Helen~~.
- *I'm* Helen.   **NOT**   ~~Am Helen~~.

> 🔍 **Negative contractions**
> I am not = I'm not
> You are not = You aren't **OR** You're not

🔊 **1.5** Listen and repeat the examples. Then read the rules.

?	+	−
Am I in class 2?	Yes, **you are**.	No, **you aren't**.
Are you Mike?	Yes, **I am**.	No, **I'm not**.

> 🔍 **Word order in questions**
> + **I'm** in class 2.   **You're** Tom.
> ? **Am I** in class 2?   **Are you** Tom?

1B verb *be* (singular): *he, she, it*

🔊 **1.22** Listen and repeat the **examples**. Then read the rules.

Full form	Contraction
+ I am from the USA.	I'm from the USA.
You are from Germany.	You're from Germany.
He is from Italy.	**He's** from Italy.
She is from Spain.	**She's** from Spain.
It is from China.	**It's** from China.

- he = man   she = woman   it = thing

🔊 **1.23** Listen and repeat the **examples**. Then read the rules.

Full form	Contraction
+ I am not from England.	I'm not from England.
You are not from Poland.	You aren't from Poland.
He is not from Egypt.	**He isn't** from Egypt.
She is not from Brazil.	**She isn't** from Brazil.
It is not from Japan.	**It isn't** from Japan.

> 🔍 **Negative contractions**
> He is not = He isn't **OR** He's not

🔊 **1.24** Listen and repeat the **examples**. Then read the rules.

?	+	−
Am I in class 2?	Yes, you are.	No, you aren't.
Are you from Russia?	Yes, I am.	No, I'm not.
Is he from France?	Yes, **he is**.	No, **he isn't**.
Is she from Turkey?	Yes, **she is**.	No, **she isn't**.
Is it good?	Yes, **it is**.	No, **it isn't**.

> 🔍 **Word order in questions**
> + **She's** from Russia.
> ? **Is she** from Russia?
> ? With *What* and *Where*:
>   What's your name? Where are you from?
>   Where's he from?

1A

a Complete with *I'm* or *You're*.

Hello. *I'm* Maria. What's your name?
1 Hi. _____ Tony. 
2 Hello. _____ your teacher. _____ in my class. 
3 _____ in class 4. 
4 _____ in room 3. 

b Complete with *I'm not* or *You aren't*.

I'm not Tom. I'm Tony.
1 _____ in class 5. You're in class 4. 
2 _____ in room 6. You're in room 7. 
3 _____ Marina. I'm Marisa. 

c Make questions.

You're Sam. *Are you Sam*?
1 I'm in room 4. _____?
2 You're Silvia. _____?
3 I'm in class 3. _____?

d Complete the conversations. Use contractions where possible.

A Hello. *Are* you Liz? B No, *I'm* not. I'm Maria.
1 A _____ I in room 8? B No, you _____. You're in room 6.
2 A _____ you in class 4? B No, I _____. I'm in class 5.
3 A _____ you Henry? B Yes, I _____. Nice to meet you!
4 A _____ I in your class? B Yes, you _____. I _____ your teacher.

← p.6

1B

a Complete with *He's*, *She's*, or *It's*.

A Where's London?
B *It's* in England.
1 A Where's Lisa from?
  B _____ from Germany.
2 A Where's Ankara?
  B _____ in Turkey.
3 A Where's Mario from?
  B _____ from Brazil.
4 A Where's St Petersburg?
  B _____ in Russia.
5 A Where's Charles from?
  B _____ from England.
6 A Where's Anne from?
  B _____ from Switzerland.
7 A Where's Benidorm?
  B _____ in Spain.
8 A Where's Carlos from?
  B _____ from Mexico.

b Complete with *is*, *'s*, or *isn't*.

A *Is* Ana from Mexico? B No, she *isn't*. She *'s* from Spain.
1 A Where _____ Osaka? _____ it in Japan?
  B Yes, it _____.
2 A _____ Mark from the USA?
  B No, he _____ from England.
3 A Where _____ she from? B She _____ from Rio.
4 A _____ Ivan from Poland?
  B No, he _____. He _____ from Russia.
5 A _____ Strasbourg in Germany?
  B No, it _____. It _____ in France.

c Complete the conversations with the correct form of *be*. Use contractions where possible.

A *Are* you from Turkey? B No, *I'm not*. I *'m* from Egypt.
1 A Where _____ Bergamo? _____ it in Italy?
  B Yes, it _____.
2 A Where _____ Alex from? _____ he from Mexico?
  B No, he _____. He _____ from the USA.
3 A Where _____ you from?
  B I _____ from Cambridge.
4 A What _____ your name?
  B My name _____ Ana. _____ from Chicago.
  A You _____ from Chicago! I _____ from Chicago, too! It _____ a great city.

← p.8

Go online to review the grammar for each lesson

GRAMMAR BANK

2A verb *be* (plural): *we, you, they*

2.6 Listen and repeat the examples. Then read the rules.

	Full form	Contraction
be +	I am English.	I'm English.
	You are Swiss.	You're Swiss.
	He is Spanish.	He's Spanish.
	She is Turkish.	She's Turkish.
	It is Japanese.	It's Japanese.
	We are American.	We're American.
	You are Egyptian.	You're Egyptian.
	They are German.	They're German.

- *you* = singular and plural

- *they* = men, women, and things

2.7 Listen and repeat the examples. Then read the rules.

	Full form	Contraction
be –	I am not English.	I'm not English.
	You are not Swiss.	You aren't Swiss.
	He is not Spanish.	He isn't Spanish.
	She is not Turkish.	She isn't Turkish.
	It is not Japanese.	It isn't Japanese.
	We are not American.	We aren't American.
	You are not Egyptian.	You aren't Egyptian.
	They are not German.	They aren't German.

> **Negative contractions**
> We are not = We aren't **OR** We're not
> You are not = You aren't **OR** You're not
> They are not = They aren't **OR** They're not

2.8 Listen and repeat the examples. Then read the rules.

be plural, ? and short answers

?	+	–
Am I in room 2?	Yes, you are.	No, you aren't.
Are you Linda?	Yes, I am.	No, I'm not.
Is he Brazilian?	Yes, he is.	No, he isn't.
Is she from Italy?	Yes, she is.	No, she isn't.
Is it good?	Yes, it is.	No, it isn't.
Are we late?	Yes, you are.	No, you aren't.
Are you from Russia?	Yes, we are.	No, we aren't.
Are they Mexican?	Yes, they are.	No, they aren't.

> **Word order in questions**
> + They're from Russia.
> ? Are they from Russia?

2B *Wh-* and *How* questions with *be*

2.18 Listen and repeat the examples. Then read the rules.

Question word(s)	Verb	Subject	
Who	's	Tom?	He's a friend.
What	's	your email?	johng@gmail.com.
Where	are	you from?	I'm from Brighton in England.
When	's	the concert?	It's on Tuesday.
How	are	you?	I'm fine, thanks.
How old	is	she?	She's ten.

> **Word order**
> + Subject, verb — They're American.
> ? Verb, subject — Are they American?
> ? Question, verb, subject — Where are they from?
>
> **Contractions with question words**
> We can contract *is* after question words.
> What's her name? = What is her name?
> Where's he from? = Where is he from?
> How's Anna? = How is Anna?
> How old's Jan? = How old is Jan?
>
> Don't contract *is* in a question when the last word is a pronoun (*he, she, it,* etc.).
> How old is she? **NOT** ~~How old's she?~~
> Where is he? **NOT** ~~Where's he?~~

2A

a Change the **bold** word(s) to a pronoun: *you, he, she, it, we, they.*

Anna and **Tom** are from London.   *They*'re from London.
1. **Diana and I** are in room 4.   _____'re in room 4.
2. **The Taj Mahal** is in India.   _____'s in India.
3. Are **Mark and James** in Italy?   Are _____ in Italy?
4. Where is **Rosa** from?   Where's _____ from?
5. **Mira and Rita** are Brazilian.   _____'re Brazilian.
6. **Paul** isn't in the hotel.   _____ isn't in the hotel.
7. **You and Sara** are in class 2.   _____'re in class 2.
8. **Jim and I** are from Oxford.   _____'re from Oxford.
9. **Honda and Toyota** are Japanese.   _____'re Japanese.

b Make ⊞ or ⊟ sentences, or ❓. Use *we, you,* or *they.*

Luisa and I / Brazilian   ⊞ *We're Brazilian.*
You and Henry / teachers   ⊟ *You aren't teachers.*
/ Liz and Tom / in Egypt   ❓ *Are they in Egypt?*
1. Ana and I / Mexican   ⊟ _____
2. You, Max, and John / in class 4   ⊞ _____
3. / Mike and Peter / English   ❓ _____
4. / Linda and I / in class 4   ❓ _____
5. You and Lucy / in class 4   ⊟ _____
6. Lucy and I / on holiday   ⊞ _____

c Complete the conversations. Use contractions where possible.

They *aren't* French. They *'re* Swiss, from Lausanne.
1. **A** _____ you from the United States?
   B No, we _____ American. We _____ English.
2. **A** _____ they Spanish?
   B Yes, they _____. They _____ from Madrid.
3. Nikolai is from Moscow. He _____ from St Petersburg.
4. Sorry, you _____ in room 20, you're in room 22.
5. **A** _____ Adidas American?
   B No, it _____, it _____ German.
6. **A** _____ we late?
   B Yes, you _____. It _____ 9.30!
7. I _____ Sara Smith, I'm Sara Simpson.
8. They _____ from New York, they're from Texas.
9. **A** Where's Laura from?
   B She _____ from Recife.
   A _____ Recife in Brazil?
   B Yes, it _____.

← p.12

2B

a Complete with a question word.

How   How old   What (x2)   When
Where (x2)   Who (x2)

A *How* are you?
B Fine, thanks. And you?
1. **A** _____'s the concert?
   B On Tuesday at 7.30.
   A _____ is it?
   B In the Festival Hall.
2. **A** _____'s your name?
   B Jessica.
3. **A** _____ is she?
   B She's my friend, Julia.
   A _____'s she from?
   B Italy.
4. **A** _____'s your email?
   B It's jbl098@yoohoo.com.
5. **A** _____'s that?
   B My brother Adrian.
   A _____ is he?
   B He's 25.

b Order the words to make questions.

are how old you?   *How old are you?*
1. she who is?   _____
2. what phone your number is?   _____
3. is where room 4?   _____
4. married is Marta?   _____
5. your English class is when?   _____
6. your number is phone 4960362?   _____
7. is his email what?   _____
8. Pedro how is old?   _____

c Write questions to complete the conversation.

A *What's your name*?   **B** Pedro Guzman.
A [1]_____?   **B** Monterrey.
A [2]_____ Monterrey?   **B** It's in Mexico.
A [3]_____?   **B** pguzman@gmail.com.
A Thanks. [4]_____?   **B** 81 8150 9304.
A [5]_____?   **B** I'm 19.

← p.14

Go online to review the grammar for each lesson

3 GRAMMAR BANK

3A singular and plural nouns; a / an

🔊 3.3 Listen and repeat the examples. Then read the rules.

Singular nouns; a / an

What is it? It's **a** book.
It's **a** key. 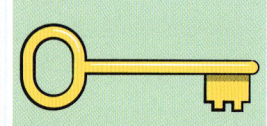
It's **an** umbrella. 
It's **an** ID card. 

- *What is it?* **NOT** *What's it?*
- We use *a / an* + singular noun.
- We use *a* + word beginning with a consonant, e.g. *a bag, a phone*.
- We use *an* + word beginning with a vowel, e.g. *an umbrella*.

🔊 3.4 Listen and repeat the examples. Then read the rules.

Singular nouns; a / an

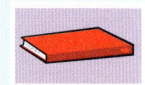

What is it? It's **a** book.   What are they? They're book**s**.
What is it? It's **a** key.   What are they? They're key**s**.
What is it? It's **a** watch.   What are they? They're watch**es**.
What is it? It's **a** dictionary.   What are they? They're dictionar**ies**.

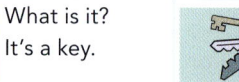

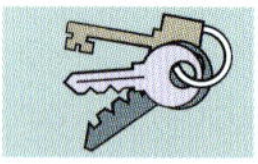

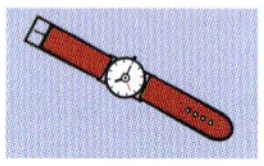

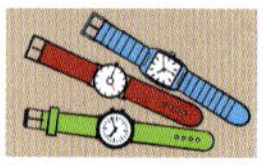

Spelling rules

	Singular	Plural	
1	a bag a holiday	bag**s** holiday**s**	add *-s*
2	a class	class**es** /ɪz/	add *-es* (after *ch, sh, s, ss, x*)
3	a country	countr**ies**	consonant + *y* = *y* -*ies*

🔍 **the**
Look at **the** board. Open **the** door. Close **the** windows.
We use *the* + singular or plural nouns, e.g. *the door, the windows*.

3B this / that / these / those

🔊 3.14 Listen and repeat the examples. Then read the rules.

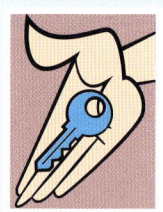

What's **this**? It's a key.
What are **these**? They're keys. 
What's **that**? It's a cat. 
What are **those**? They're cats. 

- We use *this / these* for things near you (things here).
- We use *that / those* for things that aren't near you (things there or over there).
- *this / that* = singular, *these / those* = plural.
- We also use *this / that / these / those* for people, e.g. *This is my brother. Who are those girls over there?*

🔍 **this, that, these, those**
This, that, these, and *those* are pronouns or adjectives.
This is my book. (= pronoun)
This book is very nice. (= adjective)

here, there, over there

here    there    over there

3A

a Complete the chart.

Singular	Plural
It's a pen.	They're pens.
1 _____.	They're phones.
2 It's a watch.	_____.
3 _____.	They're umbrellas.
4 It's a dictionary.	_____.
5 It's a key.	_____.
6 It's a city.	_____.
7 _____.	They're emails.
8 It's a passport.	_____.
9 _____.	They're tablets.

b Write questions and answers.

What is it?   *It's a laptop*.

1 _____?   _____.

2 _____?   _____.

3 _____?   _____.

4 _____?   _____.

5 _____?   _____.

← p.18

3B

a Look at the pictures. Complete the sentences with *this*, *that*, *these*, or *those*.

This isn't a very good book.

1 Are _____ your T-shirts?

2 _____ are my children.

3 **A** Is _____ your phone over there?
   B No, my phone's here.

4 Look at _____! They're great!

5 Who's _____? Is he your brother?

b Look at the pictures. (Circle) the correct word(s).

Meg What is (this) / that?
Joe ¹ They're / It's a key ring from New York.
Meg Oh, OK.
Joe And ² these / those are sunglasses. ³ It's / They're great!

Meg Are ⁴ these / those mugs?
Joe Yes, ⁵ it is / they are. For our coffee. And ⁶ that / this is a plate for Jenny.
Meg What ⁷ 's that / are those?
Joe ⁸ It's / They're a T-shirt. It's for you!
Meg Oh...thanks.

← p.21

Go online to review the grammar for each lesson

4 GRAMMAR BANK

4A possessive adjectives; possessive 's

🔊 **4.9** Listen and repeat the examples. Then read the rules.

Possessive adjectives	
I'm from Spain.	My name is Ana.
You're English.	Your name is Ben.
He's from Rome.	His name is Marco.
She's Italian.	Her name is Clara.
It's a French restaurant.	Its name is Chez Marcelle.
We're from Brazil.	Our names are Selma and Luis.
You're Polish.	Your names are Marek and Ania.
They're from Mexico.	Their names are Pedro and Maria.

- your names, our books, their coats **NOT** yours names, ours books, theirs coats
- its = for things or animals, e.g.
  Pizzeria Marco is a good restaurant. **Its** phone number is 0543387.
  Senegal is in Africa. **Its** flag is red, yellow, and green.
  Look at that fish! **Its** eyes are yellow.

> **It's or its?**
> It's = it is   **It's** a French restaurant.
> Its = possessive   **Its** name is Chez Marcelle.

🔊 **4.10** Listen and repeat the examples. Then read the rules.

Possessive 's
This is Jack's car.
Ella is Ben's wife.
Maria is Carlos's sister.
My sister's name is Molly.
This is my parents' house.

- We use 's after a person to talk about family and things, e.g. Ann's brother, Jim's car.
- We use ' after plural people, e.g. my brothers' room (= two brothers).

> **'s**
> She's American. Her name's Emma. ('s = is)
> Emma is Maria's daughter. ('s = possessive s)
>
> **pronunciation of 's**
> 's usually = /s/, e.g. Jack's or /z/, e.g. Maria's.
> 's after a name that ends in s = /ɪz/, e.g. Carlos's = /ˈkɑːlɒsɪz/.

4B adjectives

🔊 **4.19** Listen and repeat the examples. Then read the rules.

1. An Audi is **expensive**. It's **fast**.
2. An Audi is an **expensive** car. It's a **fast car**.
3. They're **old houses**. My **glasses** are **new**.
4. He's **tall**. She's **tall**, too.

1 We use adjectives after the verb be, e.g.
An Audi is expensive. **NOT** An Audi expensive is.

2 We use adjectives before a noun, e.g.
It's a fast car. **NOT** It's a car fast.

3 Adjectives are the same for singular and plural:
It's an old house. They're old houses. **NOT** They're olds houses.

4 Adjectives are the same for 👨 and 👩.

4A

a Complete with *my*, *your* (sing.), *his*, *her*, *its*, *your* (pl.), *our*, or *their*.

I'm American. *My* name is William.
1. They're from France. _____ names are Claire and Françoise.
2. **A** What's _____ name?
   B I'm Julia. Nice to meet you.
3. He's Italian. _____ name is Roberto.
4. It's a good hotel, and _____ restaurant is fantastic.
5. They're Mexican. _____ surname is Romero.
6. I know a very good restaurant in Paris. _____ name is Café des Fleurs.
7. _____ name is Tina. She's Brazilian.
8. Lisa and Amy are American, but _____ husbands are British.
9. **A** We're Jane and Mark Kelley. We have a reservation.
   B You're in room 22. This is _____ key.
10. Here are _____ coffees. The cappuccino is for you, the latte is for Tom, and the Americano is for me.
11. I'm Sally, and this is _____ husband, Tom.
12. **A** Are those your children?
    B No, they aren't. _____ children are over there.

b Write sentences about Sam's family. Use the names and *'s*.

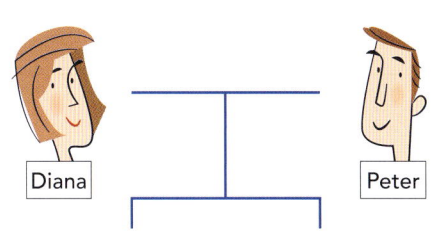

Karen / Sam — *Karen is Sam's sister.*
1. Peter / Karen _____
2. Diana / Sam _____
3. Karen / Peter _____
4. Peter / Diana _____
5. Sam / Peter _____
6. Diana / Peter _____
7. Sam / Karen _____

← p.24

4B

a Write sentences with *It's a / an* or *They're* + adjective + noun.

(great) *It's a great restaurant.*
1. (old) _____ 
2. (black) _____ 
3. (new) _____ 
4. (big) _____ 
5. (expensive) _____ 
6. (good) _____ 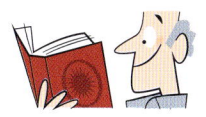

b Order the words to make sentences.

blue is bag my — *My bag is blue.*
1. beautiful a day it's _____
2. is husband nice very Amy's _____
3. questions difficult they're very _____
4. phone cheap a is this _____
5. photo it's terrible a _____
6. Maggie teacher is fantastic a _____
7. very is cat old our _____
8. restaurant this good a very isn't _____
9. long it's a exercise very _____
10. is ugly very dog their _____
11. expensive Italian bags are very _____
12. very this is small room a _____

← p.27

Go online to review the grammar for each lesson

99

5 GRAMMAR BANK

5A present simple + and −: I, you, we, they

5.5 Listen and repeat the examples. Then read the rules.

+	−
I have cereal for breakfast.	I don't have eggs for breakfast. (don't = do not)
You have rice for lunch.	You don't have pasta for lunch.
We have coffee for breakfast.	We don't have tea for breakfast.
They have fish for dinner.	They don't have meat for dinner.

- We use the present simple to talk about present habits (= things we usually do), e.g. *I have coffee for breakfast* and things that are always true, e.g. *In my country, we eat a lot of rice.*
- Present simple + and − is the same for *I, you* (singular and plural), *we*, and *they*.
- We make − sentences with *don't*, e.g. *We don't have coffee.* **NOT** *We not have coffee.*

They have fish for dinner.

5B present simple ?: I, you, we, they

5.12 Listen and repeat the examples. Then read the rules.

?	+	−
Do I need a ticket?	Yes, you do.	No, you don't.
Do you live near here?	Yes, I do.	No, I don't.
Do we have good seats?	Yes, we do.	No, we don't.
Do they like children?	Yes, they do.	No, they don't.

- Present simple ? is the same for *I, you* (singular and plural), *we*, and *they*.
- We use *do* to make questions: *Do you live here?* **NOT** *You live here?* **OR** *Live you here?*
- Remember **ASI** to help you with word order in present simple questions: **A** = auxiliary (*do*), **S** = subject (*you, they,* etc.), **I** = infinitive.

Do I need a ticket?

5A

a Write + or − sentences.

We (have) — *We have sandwiches* for lunch.

I (not like) — *I don't like fish*.

1. I (have) _____ for breakfast.
2. We (not drink) _____ in the evening.
3. They (like) _____.
4. You (eat) _____.
5. We (eat) _____ in the evening.
6. I (not have) _____ in my coffee.
7. You (not like) _____.
8. The children (eat) _____.

b Complete with the **bold** verb. Write one + sentence and one − sentence.

like
I'm Italian, but I *don't like* pasta.
My friends and I *like* fast food, especially pizzas and burgers.

1. **have**
People in the UK _____ a big lunch – they usually have a sandwich.
We always _____ lunch with my family on Sundays.

2. **eat**
I _____ meat. I'm a vegetarian.
They _____ a lot of fish and rice in Japan.

3. **drink**
You _____ a lot of coffee! It isn't good for you.
They _____ coffee. They only drink tea.

4. **go**
We _____ to restaurants. They're very expensive.
I don't have breakfast at home. I _____ to a café.

← p.31

5B

a Complete with *do* or *don't*.

I *don't* live here. I live in the centre.

1. A _____ you have children?
   B No, I _____.
2. I _____ like this photo. It's terrible.
3. A _____ you want a coffee?
   B No, thanks. I _____ drink coffee.
4. I _____ have brothers and sisters. I'm an only child.
5. A _____ you listen to music on the radio?
   B I _____ listen to pop music, but I listen to Classic FM. It's a classical music station.
6. A Excuse me, _____ you work here?
   B No, I _____. Sorry.
7. A _____ you like American TV series?
   B No, I _____. I _____ watch TV. I read.
8. A _____ you have a big family?
   B Yes, I _____. I have two brothers and three sisters.
9. A _____ you speak Spanish?
   B No, I _____. I only speak English.
10. A _____ you like Saturdays?
    B Yes, I _____. I _____ work at the weekend.

b Order the words to make sentences or questions.

umbrella have do you an? *Do you have an umbrella?*

1. know don't I. _____
2. here you near do live? _____
3. like I football don't. _____
4. sandwich want you a do? _____
5. centre work in the they city. _____
6. sisters two have I. _____
7. French you speak do? _____
8. don't big need a I car. _____
9. German to classes you do go? _____
10. a don't I watch have. _____
11. to in the music car listen you do? _____
12. work I don't Sundays on _____

← p.32

Go online to review the grammar for each lesson

6 GRAMMAR BANK

6A present simple: *he, she, it*

▶ 6.5 Listen and repeat the examples. Then read the rules.

+	−	?	+	−
I work.	I don't work.	Do I work?	Yes, I do.	No, I don't.
You work.	You don't work.	Do you work?	Yes, I do.	No, I don't.
He works.	He doesn't work.	Does he work?	Yes, he does.	No, he doesn't.
She works.	She doesn't work.	Does she work?	Yes, she does.	No, she doesn't.
It works.	It doesn't work.	Does it work?	Yes, it does.	No, it doesn't.
We work.	We don't work.	Do we work?	Yes, we do.	No, we don't.
You work.	You don't work.	Do you work?	Yes, you do.	No, you don't.
They work.	They don't work.	Do they work?	Yes, they do.	No, they don't.

- Present simple + *he / she / it* = verb + *s*.
- Present simple − *he / she / it* = *doesn't* + verb (*doesn't* = *does not*).
- Present simple ? *he / she / it* = *Does* + *he / she / it* + verb. Remember **ASI** (see **5B** p.100).

Spelling rules 3rd person *s*		
I work in an office. I live in Spain.	He works in an office. He lives in Spain.	+ *s*
I watch CNN. I finish work at 8.00.	She watches CNN. The film finishes at 8.00.	+ *es* (after *ch, sh, s, ss, x*)
I study history.	He studies history.	consonant + *y* = ~~y~~ -*ies*

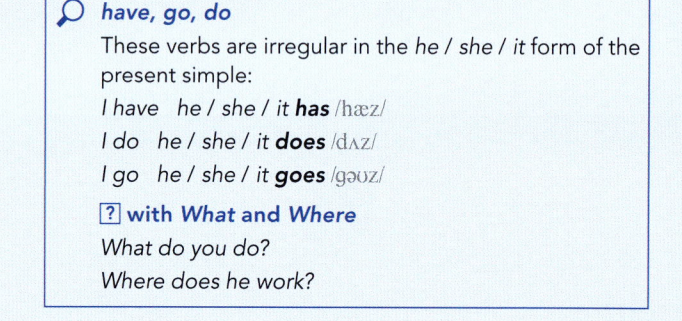

🔍 **have, go, do**
These verbs are irregular in the *he / she / it* form of the present simple:
I **have**   he / she / it **has** /hæz/
I **do**   he / she / it **does** /dʌz/
I **go**   he / she / it **goes** /ɡəʊz/

? with *What* and *Where*
What do you do?
Where does he work?

- Spelling rules for 3rd person *s* are the same as for plural nouns.

6B adverbs of frequency

▶ 6.16 Listen and repeat the examples. Then read the rules.

I **always** have breakfast.
They **usually** finish work at 5.00.
She **sometimes** watches TV in the evening.
He **never** eats meat.
Does she **usually** go shopping on Saturday?
What time do you **usually** get up?

100% always
usually
sometimes
0% never

- Be careful with the position of adverbs of frequency:
  I always have breakfast. **NOT** ~~Always I have breakfast. I have always breakfast.~~
  Does she usually go shopping on Saturday? **NOT** ~~Does usually she go shopping on Saturday? Usually does she go shopping on Saturday?~~
- With *never*, we use a + verb: He never eats meat.
  NOT ~~He doesn't never eat meat.~~

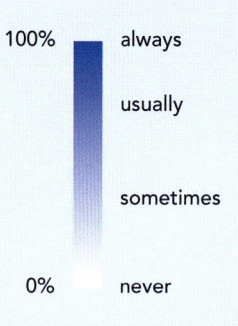

He never eats meat.

6A

a Rewrite the sentences.

I live in a flat.   She *lives in a flat*.
1. They read magazines.
   He _____.
2. I study Italian.
   My sister _____.
3. Do you speak English?
   _____ he _____?
4. I don't eat fish.
   My brother _____.
5. Where do you work?
   Where _____ your wife _____?
6. You don't speak Italian.
   Tom _____.
7. Do you like cats?
   _____ she _____?
8. I have two brothers.
   Andrew _____.
9. What do you eat for lunch?
   What _____ he _____?
10. We watch a lot of TV.
    My mother _____.
11. What do you do?
    What _____ your son _____?
12. We don't need a new car.
    Maria _____.

b Put the verb in (brackets) in the correct form.

They *don't live* near here. (not live)
1. She _____ to the radio in the car. (listen)
2. My brother _____ to university in Manchester. (go)
3. We _____ at the weekend. (not work)
4. _____ Angela _____ with her mother? (live)
5. The programme _____ at 9.30. (finish)
6. She usually _____ fruit for breakfast. (have)
7. We _____ TV at the weekend. (not watch)
8. _____ you _____ tea or coffee? (want)
9. Where _____ your children _____ to school? (go)
10. Linda _____ meat, fish, or eggs. She's a vegan. (not eat)
11. _____ Andrew _____ his new job? (like)
12. Luisa _____ brothers or sisters. (not have)

← p.36

6B

a Order the words to complete the sentences.

drink never coffee I
I never drink coffee after dinner.
1. husband goes my sometimes
   _____ to the gym.
2. have always I
   _____ a shower in the morning.
3. usually we have
   _____ breakfast at home.
4. go I never
   _____ to bed before 12.00.
5. usually go they do
   _____ to work by bus?
6. Jan has sometimes
   _____ a sandwich for lunch.
7. close the does restaurant usually
   _____ late?
8. goes she never
   _____ shopping after work.
9. usually I do
   _____ my homework at the weekend.
10. sometimes make I
    _____ fish for dinner.

b Complete the sentences in the present simple. Use a verb from the list and the adverb in (brackets).

do   drink (x2)   eat   finish   get   go
have (x3)   speak   watch

He *never eats* meat for lunch. (never)
1. Alex _____ _____ to bed very late. (sometimes)
2. We _____ _____ housework at the weekend. (always)
3. Do you _____ _____ lunch at home at the weekend? (usually)
4. I _____ _____ a bath, I _____ _____ a shower. (never, always)
5. My sister _____ _____ up early. (always)
6. I _____ _____ English at work. (never)
7. We _____ _____ TV after dinner. (sometimes)
8. They _____ _____ coffee in the evening. (never)
9. Does your husband _____ _____ work at 7.30 p.m.? (usually)
10. We _____ _____ tea with milk, but I prefer it with lemon. (sometimes)

← p.38

> **Go online** to review the grammar for each lesson

Numbers

VOCABULARY BANK

1 0–10

a 🔊 1.8 Listen and repeat the numbers.

0 zero /ˈzɪərəʊ/
   (also 'oh' /əʊ/ in phone numbers)
1 one /wʌn/
2 two /tuː/
3 three /θriː/
4 four /fɔː/
5 five /faɪv/
6 six /sɪks/
7 seven /ˈsevn/
8 eight /eɪt/
9 nine /naɪn/
10 ten /ten/

> 🔍 **Word stress**
> zero = **ze**ro   seven = **se**ven

b Cover the words. Say the numbers.

ACTIVATION Count from 0–10 and from 10–0.

⬅ p.7

2 11–100

11–20

a 🔊 2.21 Listen and repeat the numbers.

11 eleven /ɪˈlevn/
12 twelve /twelv/
13 thirteen /θɜːˈtiːn/
14 fourteen /fɔːˈtiːn/
15 fifteen /fɪfˈtiːn/
16 sixteen /sɪksˈtiːn/
17 seventeen /ˌsevnˈtiːn/
18 eighteen /eɪˈtiːn/
19 nineteen /naɪnˈtiːn/
20 twenty /ˈtwenti/

21–100

b 🔊 2.22 Listen and repeat the numbers.

21   twenty-one /ˌtwenti ˈwʌn/
22   twenty-two /ˌtwenti ˈtuː/
30   thirty /ˈθɜːti/
33   thirty-three /ˌθɜːti ˈθriː/
40   forty /ˈfɔːti/
44   forty-four /ˌfɔːti ˈfɔː/
50   fifty /ˈfɪfti/
55   fifty-five /ˌfɪfti ˈfaɪv/
60   sixty /ˈsɪksti/
66   sixty-six /ˌsɪksti ˈsɪks/
70   seventy /ˈsevnti/
77   seventy-seven /ˌsevnti ˈsevn/
80   eighty /ˈeɪti/
88   eighty-eight /ˌeɪti ˈeɪt/
90   ninety /ˈnaɪnti/
99   ninety-nine /ˌnaɪnti ˈnaɪn/
100 a hundred /ə ˈhʌndrəd/

> 🔍 **Word stress – be careful!**
> 30 **thir**ty   13 thir**teen**   40 **for**ty   14 four**teen**, etc.

ACTIVATION Cover the words. Say the numbers.

⬅ p.15

Countries and nationalities

VOCABULARY BANK

1 COUNTRIES

a ◯ 1.18 Listen and repeat the countries.

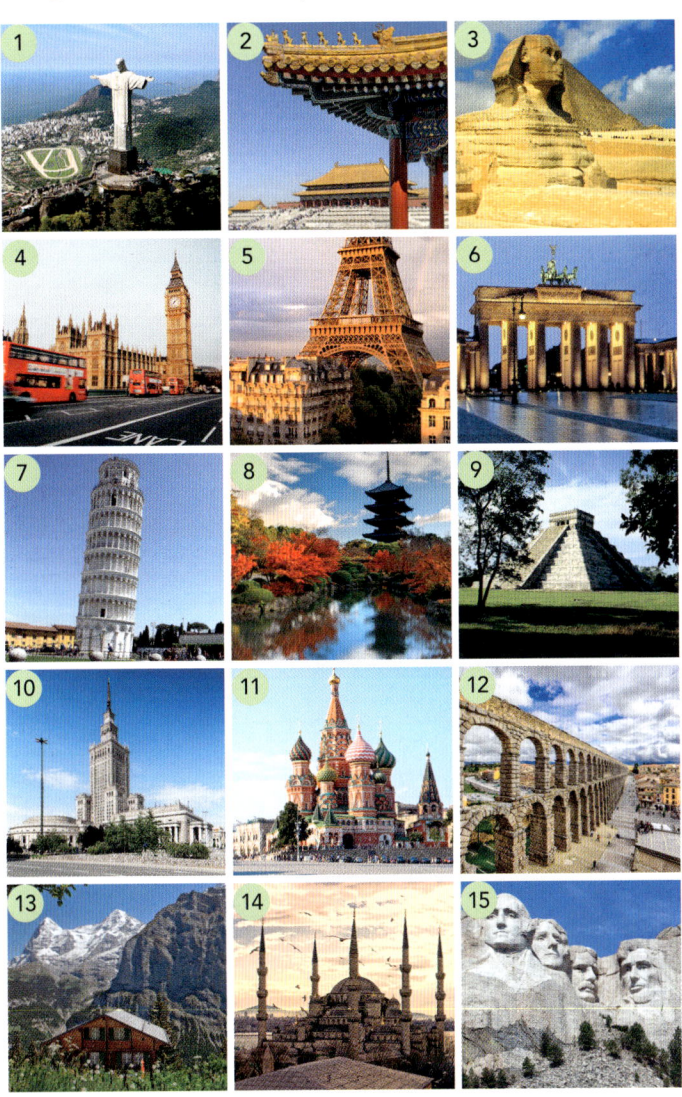

1 Brazil /brəˈzɪl/
2 China /ˈtʃaɪnə/
3 Egypt /ˈiːdʒɪpt/
4 England /ˈɪŋɡlənd/
  the UK* /ˈjuː keɪ/
5 France /frɑːns/
6 Germany /ˈdʒɜːməni/
7 Italy /ˈɪtəli/
8 Japan /dʒəˈpæn/
9 Mexico /ˈmeksɪkəʊ/
10 Poland /ˈpəʊlənd/
11 Russia /ˈrʌʃə/
12 Spain /speɪn/
13 Switzerland /ˈswɪtsələnd/
14 Turkey /ˈtɜːki/
15 the United States (the USA) /juːˈnaɪtɪd steɪts/

*the UK = England, Scotland, Wales, and Northern Ireland

> 🔎 **CAPITAL letters**
> Brazil **NOT** ~~brazil~~.

b Write your country: _____. Practise saying it.

ACTIVATION Cover the words. Look at the photos. Say the countries. ← p.8

2 NATIONALITIES

a ◯ 2.1 Listen and repeat the countries and nationalities.

Country	Nationality
Brazil	Brazilian /brəˈzɪliən/
China	Chinese /tʃaɪˈniːz/
Egypt	Egyptian /iˈdʒɪpʃn/
England	English /ˈɪŋɡlɪʃ/
France	French /frentʃ/
Germany	German /ˈdʒɜːmən/
Italy	Italian /ɪˈtæliən/
Japan	Japanese /dʒæpəˈniːz/
Mexico	Mexican /ˈmeksɪkən/
Poland	Polish /ˈpəʊlɪʃ/
Russia	Russian /ˈrʌʃn/
Spain	Spanish /ˈspænɪʃ/
Switzerland	Swiss /swɪs/
Turkey	Turkish /ˈtɜːkɪʃ/
the United States	American /əˈmerɪkən/
the UK	British /ˈbrɪtɪʃ/

> 🔎 **Word stress**
> For most countries, the word stress is the same on the country and the nationality, e.g. Brazil, Brazilian.
>
> Sometimes it's different:
> China → Chinese   Egypt → Egyptian
> Italy → Italian   Japan → Japanese

b Write your nationality: _____. Practise saying it.

c Read about countries and languages. What's the language in your country?

> 🔎 **Countries and languages**
> The word for a language is sometimes the same as the nationality.
> **England:** nationality *English*, language *English*
>
> Some are different, e.g.
> **Brazil:** nationality *Brazilian*, language *Portuguese*
> **Egypt:** nationality *Egyptian*, language *Arabic*

ACTIVATION Cover the words. Look at the flags. Say the countries and nationalities. ← p.12

◯ **Go online** to review the vocabulary for each lesson

117

The classroom

VOCABULARY BANK

1 THINGS IN THE CLASSROOM

a ◉ 1.38 Listen and repeat the words.

1 the board /bɔːd/
2 the door /dɔː/
3 a <u>wi</u>ndow /ˈwɪndəʊ/
4 a chair /tʃeə/
5 a coat /kəʊt/
6 a table /ˈteɪbl/
7 a <u>lap</u>top /ˈlæptɒp/
8 a <u>dic</u>tionary /ˈdɪkʃənri/
9 a piece of <u>pa</u>per /piːs əv ˈpeɪpə/
10 a pen /pen/
11 a bag /bæɡ/

b Cover the words. Look at the picture. Say the things.

ACTIVATION In pairs, point to things in the classroom. Your partner says the word.

What is it? It's the board.
How do you spell it? B-O-A-R-D.

2 CLASSROOM LANGUAGE

◉ 1.39 Listen and repeat the phrases.

The teacher says...

1 Look at the board, please.
2 <u>O</u>pen your books. 
3 Go to page 10. 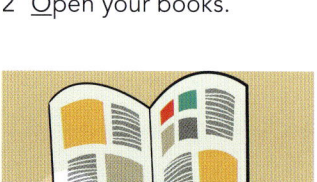 
4 Close your books. 
5 Stand up, please. 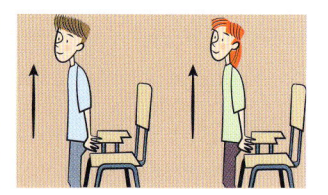
6 Sit down. 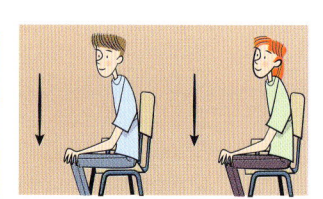

You say...

7 How do you spell it?
8 Sorry? Can you re<u>peat</u> that, please? 
9 Ex<u>cuse</u> me. What's *gracias* in <u>E</u>nglish? 
10 I don't under<u>stand</u>.
11 I don't know.
12 Sorry I'm late. 

ACTIVATION Cover the phrases. Look at the pictures. Say the phrases.

◉ p.10

Small things

VOCABULARY BANK

a 🔊 3.1 Listen and repeat the words.

1. a (mobile) phone /fəʊn/
2. a watch /wɒtʃ/
3. a tablet /ˈtæblət/
4. a wallet /ˈwɒlɪt/
   a purse /pɜːs/
5. a pencil /ˈpensl/
6. a notebook /ˈnəʊtbʊk/
7. glasses /ˈɡlɑːsɪz/
8. a photo /ˈfəʊtəʊ/
9. a (phone) charger /ˈtʃɑːdʒə/
10. an ID card /aɪˈdiː kɑːd/
    a passport /ˈpɑːspɔːt/
11. an umbrella /ʌmˈbrelə/
12. a camera /ˈkæmərə/
13. a credit card /ˈkredɪt kɑːd/
    a debit card /ˈdebɪt kɑːd/
14. a key /kiː/
15. a newspaper /ˈnjuːzpeɪpə/

> 🔍 **a / an**
> **a** bag, **a** key
> **an** ID card, **an** umbrella
>
> **ph**
> ph = /f/, e.g. **ph**one, **ph**oto

b Cover the words. Look at the photo. Say the things.

← p.18

Go online to review the vocabulary for each lesson

People and family

VOCABULARY BANK

1 PEOPLE

a 🔊 **4.2** Listen and repeat the words.

1 a boy /bɔɪ/
2 a girl /gɜːl/
3 a man /mæn/
4 a woman /ˈwʊmən/
5 children /ˈtʃɪldrən/
6 friends /frendz/

b 🔊 **4.3** Listen and repeat the irregular plurals.

> 🔍 **Irregular plurals**
> | Singular | Plural |
> |---|---|
> | a child | children |
> | a man | men |
> | a woman | women |
> | a person | people |

ACTIVATION Look at the photos in **a**. Say the words in singular and plural.

(a boy   boys

2 FAMILY

🔊 **4.4** Listen and repeat the words.

1 husband /ˈhʌzbənd/
2 wife /waɪf/
3 mother /ˈmʌðə/
4 father /ˈfɑːðə/
5 son /sʌn/
6 daughter /ˈdɔːtə/
7 brother /ˈbrʌðə/
8 sister /ˈsɪstə/
9 grandmother /ˈɡrænmʌðə/
10 grandfather /ˈɡrænfɑːðə/
11 boyfriend /ˈbɔɪfrend/
12 girlfriend /ˈɡɜːlfrend/

> 🔍 **parents**
> mother + father = parents /ˈpeərənts/ **NOT** fathers
> grandmother + grandfather = grandparents /ˈɡrænpeərənts/

ACTIVATION Cover the words. Look at the photos. Say the family members.

→ p.24

Adjectives

VOCABULARY BANK

1 COLOURS

🔊 4.16 Listen and repeat the words.

1. black /blæk/
2. blue /bluː/
3. brown /braʊn/
4. green /griːn/
5. grey /greɪ/
6. orange /ˈɒrɪndʒ/
7. pink /pɪŋk/
8. red /red/
9. white /waɪt/
10. yellow /ˈjeləʊ/

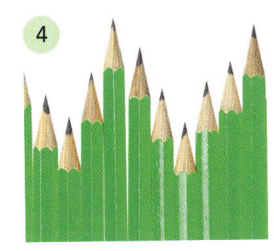

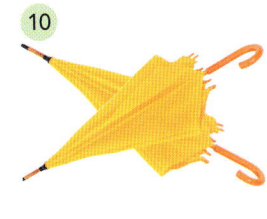

ACTIVATION Cover the words. Look at the photos. Ask and answer.

What colour is it? — *It's black.*
What colour are they? — *They're blue.*

2 COMMON ADJECTIVES

a 🔊 4.17 Listen and repeat the words.

1. big /bɪg/
2. small /smɔːl/
3. old /əʊld/
4. new /njuː/
5. fast /fɑːst/
6. slow /sləʊ/
7. beautiful /ˈbjuːtɪfl/
8. ugly /ˈʌgli/
9. cheap /tʃiːp/
10. expensive /ɪkˈspensɪv/
11. long /lɒŋ/
12. short /ʃɔːt/
13. clean /kliːn/
14. dirty /ˈdɜːti/
15. easy /ˈiːzi/
16. difficult /ˈdɪfɪkəlt/

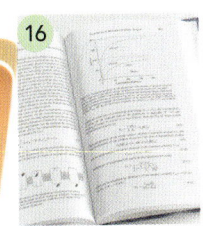

b Cover the words. Look at the photos. Say the adjectives.

ACTIVATION Test a partner.

What's the opposite of new? — *Old. What's the opposite of _____ ?*

d 🔊 4.18 Listen and repeat the positive and negative adjectives.

> 🔍 **Positive and negative adjectives**
> ✓ = good ✓✓ = very good ✓✓✓ = great / fantastic
> ✗ = bad ✗✗ = very bad ✗✗✗ = awful / terrible
>
> **very**
> You can use **very** before adjectives, e.g. *A Ferrari is **very** expensive. It's a **very** fast car.*

← p.26

Go online to review the vocabulary for each lesson

Food and drink

VOCABULARY BANK

a **5.2** Listen and repeat the words.

Food

1 fish /fɪʃ/
2 meat /miːt/ 
3 pasta /ˈpæstə/ 
4 rice /raɪs/ 
5 eggs /egz/ 
6 yogurt /ˈjɒgət/ 
7 vegetables /ˈvedʒtəblz/ 
8 potatoes /pəˈteɪtəʊz/ 
9 salad /ˈsæləd/ 
10 fruit /fruːt/ 
11 bread /bred/ 
12 butter /ˈbʌtə/ 
13 cheese /tʃiːz/ 
14 sugar /ˈʃʊgə/ 
15 a sandwich /ˈsænwɪtʃ/ 
16 cereal /ˈsɪəriəl/ 
17 chocolate /ˈtʃɒklət/ 

Drinks

18 coffee /ˈkɒfi/
19 tea /tiː/ 
20 milk /mɪlk/ 
21 water /ˈwɔːtə/  
22 orange juice /ˈɒrɪndʒ dʒuːs/ 
23 wine /waɪn/ 
24 beer /bɪə/ 

b **5.3** Listen and repeat the words and phrases in the box.

ACTIVATION Cover the words in **a**. Look at the photos. Say the words. → p.30

> **Meals**
> breakfast (in the morning)
> lunch (in the afternoon)
> dinner (in the evening)
>
> **Verbs: have, eat, drink**
> I **have** breakfast at 8.00.
> I **have** cereal and tea.
> I **eat** a lot of fruit.
> I **drink** tea with milk.

eat

drink

Common verb phrases 1

VOCABULARY BANK

a ◘ 5.13 Listen and repeat the phrases.

1 **live** in a flat /lɪv ɪn ə flæt/

2 **have** breakfast (lunch / dinner) /hæv ˈbrekfəst/ (lʌntʃ / ˈdɪnə/

3 **watch** TV /wɒtʃ tiːˈviː/

4 **listen** to the radio /ˈlɪsn tə ðə ˈreɪdiəʊ/

5 **read** the newspaper /riːd ðə ˈnjuːzpeɪpə/

6 **eat** fast food /iːt fɑːst fuːd/

7 **drink** tea /drɪŋk tiː/

8 **speak** English /spiːk ˈɪŋglɪʃ/

9 **want** a coffee /wɒnt ə ˈkɒfi/

10 **have** a dog /hæv ə dɒg/

11 **like** cats /laɪk kæts/

12 **work** in a bank /wɜːk ɪn ə bæŋk/

13 **study** Spanish /ˈstʌdi ˈspænɪʃ/

14 **go** to English classes /gəʊ tə ˈɪŋglɪʃ ˈklɑːsɪz/

15 **need** a new car /niːd ə njuː kɑː/

b ◘ 5.14 Cover the phrases. Listen and say the phrase.

1))) in a flat (live in a flat

ACTIVATION Ask and answer with a partner in a different order.

Do you drink tea? (*Yes, I do.* (*No, I don't.*

← p.33

Go online to review the vocabulary for each lesson

123

Jobs and places of work

VOCABULARY BANK

1 WHAT DO THEY DO?

a ▶ 6.1 Listen and repeat the words.

1 a <u>tea</u>cher /ˈtiːtʃə/
2 a <u>doc</u>tor /ˈdɒktə/ 
3 a nurse /nɜːs/ 
4 a <u>jour</u>nalist /ˈdʒɜːnəlɪst/ 
5 a <u>wai</u>ter /ˈweɪtə/ 
   a <u>wai</u>tress /ˈweɪtrəs/
6 a shop a<u>ssis</u>tant /ˈʃɒp əsɪstənt/ 
7 a re<u>cep</u>tionist /rɪˈsepʃənɪst/ 
8 a po<u>lice</u>man /pəˈliːsmən/ 
   a po<u>lice</u>woman /pəˈliːswʊmən/
9 a <u>fac</u>tory <u>wor</u>ker /ˈfæktəri ˈwɜːkə/ 
10 a <u>ta</u>xi <u>dri</u>ver /ˈtæksi ˈdraɪvə/ 

b Cover the words. Ask and answer in pairs.

What does he do?) (*He's a teacher.*
What does she do?) (*She's a…*

c ▶ 6.2 Listen and repeat the sentences.

I work for an A<u>me</u>rican <u>com</u>pany. /ˈkʌmpəni/
I'm at uni<u>ver</u>sity. /juːnɪˈvɜːsəti/
I'm a <u>stu</u>dent. /ˈstjuːdnt/
I study eco<u>no</u>mics. /ekəˈnɒmɪks/
I'm at school.
I'm unem<u>ployed</u> at the <u>mo</u>ment. /ʌnɪmˈplɔɪd/
I'm re<u>ti</u>red. /rɪˈtaɪəd/

d What do <u>you</u> do?

I _____.

2 WHERE DO THEY WORK?

a ▶ 6.3 Listen and repeat the phrases.

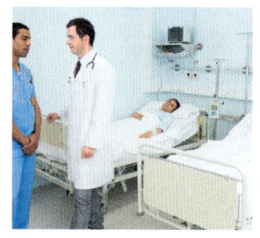

1 in a <u>hos</u>pital /ˈhɒspɪtl/
2 in a shop /ʃɒp/ 
3 in a <u>res</u>taurant /ˈrestrɒnt/ 
4 in an <u>off</u>ice /ˈɒfɪs/ 
5 in a school /skuːl/ 
6 in a <u>fac</u>tory /ˈfæktəri/ 
7 at home /həʊm/ 
8 in the street /striːt/ 

b Cover the phrases. Look at the photos. Say the phrases.

c Ask and answer with a partner.

Where does a doctor work?) (*In a hospital.*

d Where do <u>you</u> work or study?

I _____.

→ p.36

A typical day

VOCABULARY BANK

a ▶ 6.14 Listen and repeat the phrases.

IN THE MORNING

1. get up /ɡet ʌp/
2. have breakfast /hæv ˈbrekfəst/
3. have a shower /hæv ə ˈʃaʊə/
4. go to work /ɡəʊ tə wɜːk/ (by bus, train, car, etc.)
5. have a coffee /hæv ə ˈkɒfi/

IN THE AFTERNOON

6. have lunch /hæv lʌntʃ/
7. finish work /ˈfɪnɪʃ wɜːk/
8. go home /ɡəʊ həʊm/
9. go shopping /ɡəʊ ˈʃɒpɪŋ/
10. go to the gym /ɡəʊ tə ðə dʒɪm/

IN THE EVENING

11. make dinner /meɪk ˈdɪnə/
12. have dinner /hæv ˈdɪnə/
13. do housework /duː ˈhaʊswɜːk/
14. watch TV /wɒtʃ tiːˈviː/
15. have a bath /hæv ə bɑːθ/
16. go to bed /ɡəʊ tə bed/

> 🔍 **make and do**
> make dinner / coffee **BUT** do housework, do homework
>
> **go with to and the**
> go **to the** gym, go **to the** cinema
> go **to** work, go **to** school, go **to** bed
> go home **NOT** go to home

b ▶ 6.15 Listen and point to the picture.

)) *Lisa has lunch at one o'clock.* (*Picture six.*

ACTIVATION In pairs, describe Lisa's day. Say the times where there are clocks.

She gets up at a quarter to seven.) (*She has breakfast.*

← p.38

Go online to review the vocabulary for each lesson

Words and phrases to learn

1A 🔊 1.15
Hello.
Hi.
What's your name?
Nice to meet you.

A cappuccino, please.
A tea.
Yes.
No.
OK.
Thanks.
Sorry.
Just a minute.

Goodbye. / Bye.
See you on Friday.
See you tomorrow.

1B 🔊 1.31
Where are you from?
I'm from Spain.
Where's Izmir?
I think it's in Turkey.
It's a nice city.

I don't know.
Very good.
Wow!

2A 🔊 2.12
Excuse me.
Are they free?
Are you on holiday?
We're on business.
What's that?
Have a nice day!
It's a beautiful city.
tourists
dogs
over there

2B 🔊 2.27
Who's he?
How old is he?
He's very good-looking.

How are you?
I'm fine.
This is Alex.
That's my bus.
This is my bus stop.

What class are you in?
What's your phone number?
See you later.

a bedroom
a kitchen
a garden

big
small

in the south of England

3A 🔊 3.9
Oh no!
Where's my phone?
Where are my glasses?

What is it?
What are they?

I think it's an ID card.
I think they're keys.

What's in your bag?
I have two credit cards.

3B 🔊 3.17
How much is this mug?
How much are these key
  rings?
They're twenty pounds.
A T-shirt, please.

Is this your phone?
Thank you very much.
You're welcome.

souvenirs
here
there

4A 🔊 4.12
Come in.
Be good.
Let's order pizza.

on the table
in my phone

Mum
Dad
a babysitter

What a lovely card!
Can I see?
I remember.
perhaps

4B 🔊 4.24
sir
madam

an electric car
a sports car

easy to park
perfect

in her (my, your,…) opinion
Is the car for you?
I prefer this red car.
I love it!
Come with me.

a museum
a village
a motorbike
famous

5A 🔊 5.10
a scientist
a doctor

sometimes
usually

I'm not hungry.
early
healthy
traditional
important
different
favourite

in a café
at home
at work

soup
green tea
toast
a lot of (fruit)

5B 🔊 5.20
a writer
a taxi driver
a British (American)
  company
a flight
traffic
a gate

at university
at school

Do you want fish or pasta?
How's your pasta?
I need to go to the toilet.
What time do we arrive?
Keep the change.
Can I see your passport and
  boarding pass, please?
What a nice surprise!

6A 🔊 6.11
What does she do?
Where does he teach?
She's a journalist.
She doesn't wear glasses.
Her hair's blonde.
He's married to Lisa.

Great to see you.
intelligent
How awful!
I love your shoes.

a barman
a banker
customers
dishes
a multinational company
meetings

Why? Because…

6B 🔊 6.19
Are you a morning person?
What time do you get up?
At eight o'clock.
He gets up at about 9.30.
feel tired

on the way to work
after work
every morning
then

a tour guide
an apartment
the subway
an omelette

It's delicious.

Regular and irregular verbs

COMMON REGULAR VERBS

answer /'ɑːnsə/	answered /'ɑːnsəd/
arrive /ə'raɪv/	arrived /ə'raɪvd/
ask /ɑːsk/	asked /ɑːskt/
book /bʊk/	booked /bʊkt/
carry /'kæri/	carried /'kærid/
change /tʃeɪndʒ/	changed /tʃeɪndʒd/
check in /tʃek 'ɪn/	checked in /tʃekt 'ɪn/
clean /kliːn/	cleaned /kliːnd/
close /kləʊz/	closed /kləʊzd/
cook /kʊk/	cooked /kʊkt/
cry /kraɪ/	cried /kraɪd/
decide /dɪ'saɪd/	decided /dɪ'saɪdɪd/
finish /'fɪnɪʃ/	finished /'fɪnɪʃt/
hate /heɪt/	hated /'heɪtɪd/
help /help/	helped /helpt/
invite /ɪn'vaɪt/	invited /ɪn'vaɪtɪd/
learn /lɜːn/	learned /lɜːnd/
like /laɪk/	liked /laɪkt/
listen /'lɪsn/	listened /'lɪsnd/
live /lɪv/	lived /lɪvd/
look /lʊk/	looked /lʊkt/
love /lʌv/	loved /lʌvd/
miss /mɪs/	missed /mɪst/
move /muːv/	moved /muːvd/
need /niːd/	needed /'niːdɪd/
offer /'ɒfə/	offered /'ɒfəd/
open /'əʊpən/	opened /'əʊpənd/
pack /pæk/	packed /pækt/
paint /peɪnt/	painted /'peɪntɪd/
park /pɑːk/	parked /pɑːkt/
pass /pɑːs/	passed /pɑːst/
phone /fəʊn/	phoned /fəʊnd/
play /pleɪ/	played /pleɪd/
rain /reɪn/	rained /reɪnd/
relax /rɪ'læks/	relaxed /rɪ'lækst/
rent /rent/	rented /'rentɪd/
snow /snəʊ/	snowed /snəʊd/
start /stɑːt/	started /'stɑːtɪd/
stay /steɪ/	stayed /steɪd/
stop /stɒp/	stopped /stɒpt/
study /'stʌdi/	studied /'stʌdid/
talk /tɔːk/	talked /tɔːkt/
travel /'trævl/	travelled /'trævld/
turn /tɜːn/	turned /tɜːnd/
use /juːz/	used /juːzd/
wait /weɪt/	waited /'weɪtɪd/
walk /wɔːk/	walked /wɔːkt/
want /wɒnt/	wanted /'wɒntɪd/
wash /wɒʃ/	washed /wɒʃd/
watch /wɒtʃ/	watched /wɒtʃt/
work /wɜːk/	worked /wɜːkt/

COMMON IRREGULAR VERBS

be /biː/	
am /æm/ / is /ɪz/	was /wɒz/
are /ɑː/	were /wɜː/
buy /baɪ/	bought /bɔːt/
do /duː/	did /dɪd/
get /get/	got /gɒt/
go /gəʊ/	went /went/
have /hæv/	had /hæd/
leave /liːv/	left /left/
say /seɪ/	said /sed/
see /siː/	saw /sɔː/
send /send/	sent /sent/
sit /sɪt/	sat /sæt/
tell /tel/	told /təʊld/
write /raɪt/	wrote /rəʊt/

Vowel sounds

SOUND BANK

		usual spelling		! but also
fish	i	Italy six is it film window		English women gym
tree	ee ea e	three meet please read she we		people key
cat	a	bag thanks man black bad that		
car	ar a	are park fast father afternoon		
clock	o	not from sorry stop coffee		what watch want
horse	or al aw	short important tall football draw		water four
bull	u oo	full sugar good book look cook		woman could
boot	oo u* ew	too food excuse blue new		two you juice beautiful
computer	Many different spellings, always unstressed. sister actor famous about policeman			
bird	er ir ur	person verb thirsty girl nurse Turkey		work word world
egg	e	spell ten seven twenty Mexico		friend breakfast bread
up	u	umbrella number brush husband but		son brother young

		usual spelling		! but also
train	a* ai ay	name late email Spain day say		eight they great
phone	o* oa	open close no hello coat		window
bike	i* y igh	I Hi nice bye my night right		buy
owl	ou ow	out house pound sound town down		
boy	oi oy	toilet noise boyfriend enjoy		
ear	eer ere ear	beer here we're near year		really idea cereal
chair	air ere	airport repair where there		their careful
tourist	A very unusual sound. euro Europe sure plural			
/i/	A sound between /ɪ/ and /iː/. Consonant + y at the end of words is pronounced /i/. happy angry hungry			
/u/	An unusual sound. usually situation education			

* especially before consonant + e

☐ short vowels   ☐ long vowels   ☐ diphthongs

Consonant sounds

SOUND BANK

		usual spelling		! but also
	parrot	p pp	paper Poland sleep top opposite happy	
	bag	b bb	board British remember job hobby	
	key	c k ck	colour credit card look coke back clock	chemist's
	girl	g gg	go green big blog eggs	
	flower	f ph ff	fifteen Friday wife photo phone office different	
	vase	v	TV very have live seven five	of
	tie	t tt	time tell start late letter butter	liked finished
	dog	d dd	did drink study good address middle	played cried
	snake	s ss ce/ci	sit stand Swiss actress nice city	science
	zebra	z s	zero Brazil bags cars husband easy	
	shower	sh ti	shop she Spanish finish information reservation (ti + on)	sugar sure Russia
	television	si (+ on) revision		usually garage

		usual spelling		! but also
θ	thumb	th	thing think tenth birthday month Thursday	
ð	mother	th	the father this their that with	
	chess	ch tch t (+ure)	children lunch watch match picture	
dʒ	jazz	j dge	Japan juice job bridge	gym page
	leg	l ll	lamp listen plan table small umbrella	
	right	r rr	red rice problem street terrible married	write wrong
	witch	w wh	watch twenty word we what white where	one
	yacht	y before u	yellow your yes you student university	
	monkey	m mm	museum Monday September come summer swimming	
	nose	n nn	nine never men fine beginner dinner	know
ŋ	singer	ng	thing single doing going playing wrong	think thank
	house	h	hello hi how he have holiday	who

☐ unvoiced   ☐ voiced

Go online to watch the Sound Bank videos

135

English File

Beginner Workbook A
Units 1–6

WITH KEY

fourth edition

OXFORD
UNIVERSITY PRESS

Christina Latham-Koenig
Clive Oxenden
Jerry Lambert

with Jane Hudson

Paul Seligson and Clive Oxenden
are the original co-authors of
English File 1 and *English File 2*

Contents

1

- 4 **A** A cappuccino, please
- 6 **B** World music
- 8 **Practical English** Episode 1 How do you spell it?

2

- 10 **A** Are you on holiday?
- 12 **B** That's my bus!

3

- 14 **A** Where are my keys?
- 16 **B** Souvenirs
- 18 **Practical English** Episode 2 Can I have an orange juice, please?

4

- 20 **A** Meet the family
- 22 **B** The perfect car

5

- 24 **A** A big breakfast?
- 26 **B** A very long flight
- 28 **Practical English** Episode 3 What time is it?

6

- 30 **A** A school reunion
- 32 **B** Good morning, goodnight

64 **Answer Key**

How to use your Workbook and Online Practice

English File
fourth edition

Student's Book
Use the Student's Book section in class with your teacher.

IN CLASS

AT HOME

ACTIVITIES AUDIO VIDEO RESOURCES

ONLINE

Go to **englishfileonline.com** and use the code on your Access Card to log into the Online Practice.

Workbook

Practise **Grammar**, **Vocabulary**, and **Pronunciation** for every lesson.

Online Practice

← Look again at the Grammar, Vocabulary, and Pronunciation from the Student's Book section before you do the Workbook exercises.

→ Listen to the audio for the Pronunciation exercises.

→ Use the Sound Bank videos to practise English sounds.

Practise the **Practical English** for every episode.

← Watch the Practical English videos before you do the exercises.

→ Use the interactive video for more Practical English practice.

Do the **Can you remember...?** exercises to check that you remember the Grammar, Vocabulary, and Pronunciation every two Files.

Look again at the Grammar, Vocabulary and Pronunciation if you have any problems.

Practise Reading, Listening, Speaking and Writing.

Course overview

1A A cappuccino, please

> You say goodbye, and I say hello.
> *From the song* Hello, Goodbye
> *by the Beatles*

G verb *be* (singular): *I* and *you*   **V** numbers 0–10, days of the week   **P** /h/, /aɪ/, and /iː/

1 GRAMMAR verb *be* (singular): *I* and *you*

a Write the sentences with contractions.

1 I am Tom.
   I'm Tom.
2 You are not in class 3.
   You aren't in class 3.
3 I am not Helen.
   _____
4 You are not a teacher.
   _____
5 I am Rob.
   _____
6 You are in my class.
   _____
7 I am in room 4.
   _____
8 You are not Diana.
   _____

b Write negative ⊟ sentences or questions ?.

1 You're in my class. ⊟
   You aren't in my class.
2 You're a teacher. ?
   Are you a teacher?
3 I'm Jenny. ⊟
   _____
4 I'm in class 2. ⊟
   _____
5 I'm in room 4. ?
   _____
6 You're Dom. ?
   _____
7 I'm a student. ⊟
   _____
8 You're in class 7. ?
   _____

c Complete the conversations. Use contractions where possible.

1 A *Are you* Andy?
   B No, *I'm* Tony.

2 A Excuse me. _____ in number 8?
   B Yes, _____. I'm Anna Jones.

3 A Hello, _____ Amy.
   B Hi, _____ Steve. Nice to meet you.

4 A Hi, _____ Linda. Are you Henry?
   B No, _____. I'm Max.

5 A Hello. _____ Lisa Gomez?
   B Yes, _____. Nice to meet you.

6 A Hi. _____ Ben.
   B Hi. _____ Rob.

7   A   Excuse me. _____ in room 7?
    B   No, _____. You're in room 8.

8   A   Excuse me. _____ my teacher?
    B   Yes, _____. I'm Peter Wilson.

2 VOCABULARY numbers 0–10, days of the week

a   Write the numbers.

    R U F O   f o u r
    N E T   t e n
    I N N E   n __ __ e
    E O N   o __ __
    T E R E H   t __ __ __ e
    O W T   t __ __
    G I T H E   e __ __ __ t
    X I S   s __ __
    E N V S E   s __ __ __ n
    O Z R E   z __ __ o
    V I E F   f __ __ e

b   Write the numbers from **a** in the correct order.

    0   _zero_   6   _____
    1   _____   7   _____
    2   _____   8   _____
    3   _____   9   _____
    4   _____   10 _____
    5   _____

c   Write the next day of the week.

    1   Saturday   Sunday   _Monday_
    2   Monday   Tuesday   _____
    3   Thursday   Friday   _____
    4   Sunday   Monday   _____
    5   Friday   Saturday   _____
    6   Tuesday   Wednesday _____
    7   Wednesday Thursday   _____

d   Answer the questions about you.

    1   What's your name?
        _____
    2   What class are you in?
        _____
    3   What day is it today?
        _____
    4   What days are your English classes?
        _____

3 PRONUNCIATION /h/, /aɪ/, and /iː/

a   ◉ 1.1 Listen and write the words in the chart.

    ~~five~~   Helen   hello   meet   nice   tea

1 **h**ouse	2 b**i**ke	3 tr**ee**
	five	

b   ◉ 1.2 Listen and check. Then listen again and repeat the words.

4 WORDS AND PHRASES TO LEARN

Complete the conversations with a word or phrase from the list.

Nice to meet you   ~~Two cappuccinos, please~~
Sorry   See you tomorrow   Thanks   What's your name

1   A   _Two cappuccinos, please_ .
    B   OK. Just a minute.

2   A   Hi, I'm Helen.
    B   Hi, I'm Rob. _____.

3   A   Hello, I'm Sarah. _____?
    B   Paul.

4   A   Goodbye. _____.
    B   No, Friday.
    A   Oh yes, sorry. See you on Friday.

5   A   I'm not John, I'm James.
    B   _____.

6   A   Tom? Your tea.
    B   _____.

1B World music

I am a citizen of the world.
Diogenes, Greek philosopher

G verb be (singular): he, she, it   **V** countries   **P** /t/, /əʊ/, /s/, and /ʃ/

1 VOCABULARY countries

a Complete the crossword.

ACROSS →

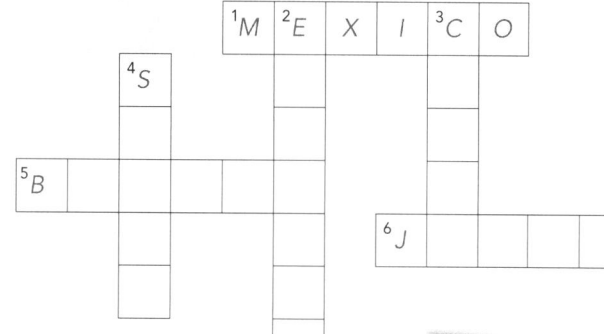

DOWN ↓

1 M 2 E X I 3 C O
4 S
5 B
6 J

b Complete the sentences with a country.
1. She's from Zurich. She's from Sw*itzerland*.
2. He's from Paris. He's from Fr_____.
3. I'm from Rome. I'm from I_____.
4. You're from Miami. You're from t____ U_____ St_____.
5. She's from Moscow. She's from R_____.
6. He's from Istanbul. He's from T_____.
7. I'm from Warsaw. I'm from P_____.
8. You're from Cairo. You're from E_____.
9. She's from Berlin. She's from G_____.

2 GRAMMAR verb be (singular): he, she, it

a Complete the sentences with He's, She's, or It's.

1. *She's* from the United States.
2. *It's* from China. 
3. _____ from Italy. 
4. _____ from Germany. 
5. _____ from Mexico. 
6. _____ from Japan. 
7. _____ from Spain. 
8. _____ from Switzerland.

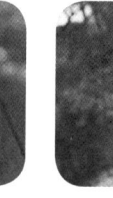

b Complete the conversations with 's, is, or isn't.

1 A <u>Is</u> Paulo from Spain?
  B No, he <u>isn't</u>. He _____ from Brazil.

2 A Where _____ Oaxaca? _____ it in Mexico?
  B Yes, it _____.

3 A _____ Yasmin in the Monday class?
  B No, she _____. She _____ in the Tuesday class.

4 A _____ your name Annie?
  B No, it _____. It _____ Anna.

c Write the questions. Then answer with the information in brackets.

1 Robert Downey Jr / from the USA? (✓ New York)
  <u>Is Robert Downey Jr from the USA</u>?
  <u>Yes, he is. He's from New York</u>.
2 Kobe / in China? (✗ Japan)
  <u>Is Kobe in China</u>?
  <u>No, it isn't. It's in Japan</u>.
3 Salma Hayek / from Mexico? (✓ Veracruz)
  _____?
  _____.
4 Naples / in Turkey? (✗ Italy)
  _____?
  _____.
5 Copacabana / in Brazil? (✓ Rio)
  _____?
  _____.
6 Lublin / in Russia? (✗ Poland)
  _____?
  _____.
7 Gary Oldman / from England? (✓ London)
  _____?
  _____.
8 Geneva / in France? (✗ Switzerland)
  _____?
  _____.
9 Javier Bardem / from Spain? (✓ Las Palmas)
  _____?
  _____.
10 the Louvre / in Italy? (✗ France)
  _____?
  _____.

d Answer the questions about you.

1 Are you from England?
  _____
2 Where are you from (city)?
  _____
3 Where is it?
  _____

3 PRONUNCIATION /ɪ/, /əʊ/, /s/, and /ʃ/

a 🔊 1.3 Listen and circle the word with a different sound.

fish	1 Brazil (China) England
phone	2 hello Poland two
snake	3 six France classroom
shower	4 Russia Spain she

b 🔊 1.3 Listen again and repeat the words.

4 WORDS AND PHRASES TO LEARN

Complete the conversations with a phrase from the list.

I don't know   I think she's from Spain   It's a nice city
~~Where are you from~~   Where's Basel

1 A <u>Where are you from</u>?
  B I'm from the United States.
  A Where in the United States?
  B New York.
  A Wow! _____.

2 A Is Mercedes Peón from Mexico?
  B No, _____.

3 A Is Sapporo in China?
  B Sapporo? Sorry, _____.

4 A _____?
  B It's in Switzerland.

Go online for more practice   7

EPISODE 1

Practical English How do you spell it?

checking into a hotel, booking a table   **V** the classroom   **P** the alphabet

1 THE ALPHABET

a 1.4 Listen and circle the letter with a different vowel sound.

iː (tree)	1 D E **I** V
e (egg)	2 E L N X
eɪ (train)	3 A G J K
iː (tree)	4 B H P D
e (egg)	5 C F L S
eɪ (train)	6 A H J Y
uː (boot)	7 O Q U W
e (egg)	8 F T M S

b 1.4 Listen again and repeat the letters.

c Say the letters in 1–5.

1. NBA
2. ID
3. JFK
4. E.T. THE EXTRA-TERRESTRIAL
5. SOS

d 1.5 Listen and check.

e 1.6 Listen and write the words in the chart.

hello help name please she spell Spain table teacher

1 tr**ee**	2 **e**gg	3 tr**ai**n
	hello	

f 1.7 Listen and check. Then listen again and repeat the words.

2 VOCABULARY the classroom

a Write the words.

1 the b_oard_
2 a l_____
3 a p_____
4 a t_____
5 the d_____
6 a ch_____
7 a w_____
8 a d_____y
9 a b_____
10 a c_____
11 a p_____ of p_____

8

b Complete the classroom expressions with the words from the list.

books Excuse Go know late Look Open
repeat Sit Stand spell understand

1 I don't *know*.
2 Sorry? Can you _____ that, please?
3 _____ at the board, please.
4 _____ your books.
5 I don't _____.
6 How do you _____ it?
7 _____ to page 9.
8 Close your _____.
9 _____ up, please.
10 _____ down.
11 _____ me. What's *grazie* in English?
12 Sorry, I'm _____.

3 CHECKING INTO A HOTEL

Complete the conversation with the words from the list.

evening name reservation spell surname room

A Good ¹*evening*.
B Hello. I have a ²_____.
A What's your ³_____, please?
B Wendy Mahoney.
A How do you ⁴_____ your ⁵_____?
B M-A-H-O-N-E-Y.
A Thank you, Ms Mahoney. You're in ⁶_____ 261.
B Thanks.

4 BOOKING A TABLE

Match the questions in the conversation to answers a–e below.

A Good morning. How can I help you?
B ¹ *b*
A What time?
B ² ____
A OK, that's fine. What's your name, please?
B ³ ____
A OK. How many people?
B ⁴ ____
A Thank you, Mr Anderson. So, a table for three on Tuesday at seven?
B ⁵ ____

a Three.
b A table for Tuesday evening, please.
c Yes, that's great. Thanks.
d Steve Anderson.
e Seven o'clock.

5 USEFUL PHRASES

Complete the conversations with a phrase from the list.

A table for tomorrow, please   Good morning
How can I help you   How do you spell it
I have a reservation   Sorry   Thank you   That's right

1 A Good morning. ¹*How can I help you*?
  B My name's Liam Sweeney. ²_____ for a room for tonight.
  A OK – Sweeney. ³_____?
  B S-W-E-E-N-E-Y.
  A That's S-W-E-E-N-E-Y?
  B ⁴_____.
  A OK, you're in room 49.

2 A ⁵_____, The Green Tree restaurant. How can I help you?
  B ⁶_____ – for four people.
  A OK. What time?
  B 7.30.
  A ⁷_____?
  B 7.30.
  A ⁸_____.

2A Are you on holiday?

> Our true nationality is mankind.
> H.G. Wells, British writer

G verb *be* (plural): *we, you, they* **V** nationalities **P** /dʒ/, /tʃ/, and /ʃ/

1 VOCABULARY nationalities

Complete the puzzle. What's the mystery word?

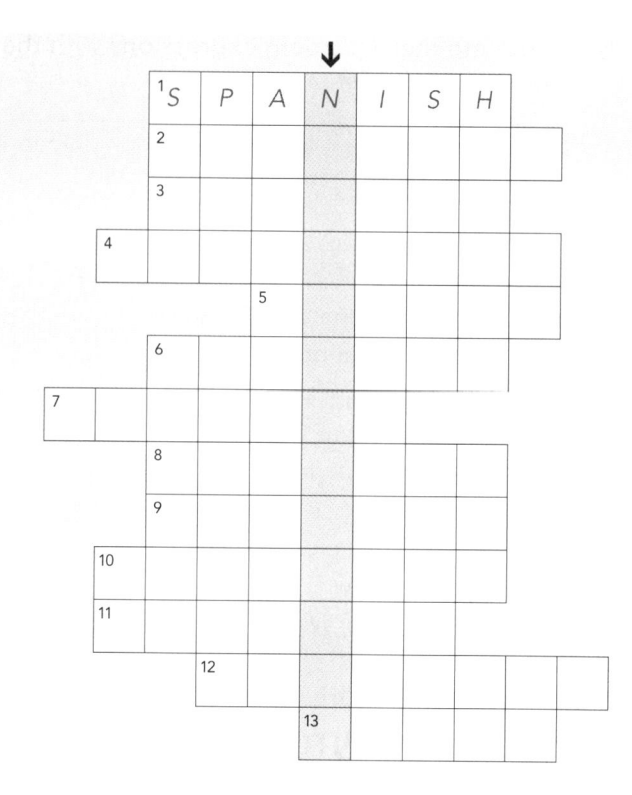

1 Maria's from Spain. She's **S**panis**h**.
2 Kentaro's from Japan. He's **J**_____**e**. 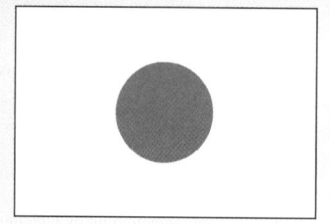
3 Emma's from the UK. She's **B**_____**h**. 
4 Bianca's from Brazil. She's **Br**_____**n**. 
5 Jacek's from Poland. He's **P**_____**h**. 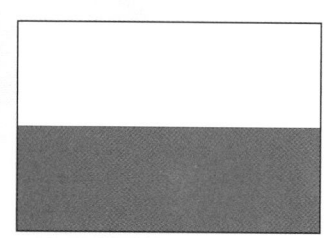
6 Meiling's from China. She's **Ch**_____**e**. 
7 Nikolay's from Russia. He's **R**_____**n**. 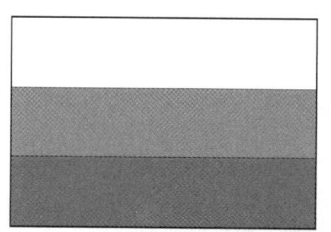
8 William's from England. He's **E**_____**h**. 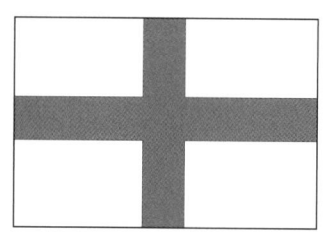
9 Daniela's from Mexico. She's **M**_____**n**. 
10 Baba's from Egypt. He's **E**_____**n**. 
11 Derin's from Turkey. She's **T**_____**h**. 
12 Mike's from the United States. He's **Am**_____**n**. 
13 Cédric's from Switzerland. He's **Sw**_____**s**. 

¹ S P A N I S H

2 PRONUNCIATION /dʒ/, /tʃ/, and /ʃ/

a 🔊 2.1 Listen and write the words in the chart.

~~Chinese~~ Egyptian French German Japanese
just Russian teacher Turkish

1 jazz	2 chess	3 shower
	Chinese	

b 🔊 2.2 Listen and check. Then listen again and repeat the words.

3 GRAMMAR verb be (plural): we, you, they

a Write positive ➕ and negative ➖ sentences with be. Use contractions.

1 we / from Spain ✓ Italy ✗
   We're from Spain. We aren't from Italy.
2 you / teachers ✓ students ✗
3 they / Chinese ✓ Japanese ✗
4 we / from Mexico ✓ Brazil ✗
5 you / in class 3 ✓ class 2 ✗
6 they / from Egypt ✓ Turkey ✗
7 she / room 4 ✓ room 5 ✗
8 I / Polish ✓ Russian ✗

b Write the sentences with pronouns. Use contractions.

1 Juan and I are from Spain.
   We're from Spain.
2 Sara and Mikel are in class 6.
3 Marina's on holiday.
4 Rodrigo's from Brazil.
5 Jake and I are here on business.
6 Toronto is in Canada.

c Re-order the words to make questions.

1 dogs they are your
   Are they your dogs?
2 class in 1 are they
   _____?
3 they England from are
   _____?
4 Italian Fernanda is
   _____?
5 in Zurich is Switzerland
   _____?

d Match the answers to the questions in c.

a _4_   Yes, she is.
b ___   No, they're in class 2.
c ___   No, they aren't.
d ___   Yes, it is.
e ___   Yes, they're from London.

e Answer the questions about your class.

1 Are you English?
   No, we aren't. We're _____.
2 Where are you from?
   _____.
3 What room are you in?
   _____.

4 WORDS AND PHRASES TO LEARN

Complete the missing words in the conversations.

1 A Excuse me. A_re_____ th_ey_____ fr_ee_____?
  B Yes, they are. Please sit down.
  A Thanks.

2 A A_____ y_____ o_____ h_____?
  B Yes, we are. We're from Spain.

3 A Your cappuccino.
  B Thanks.
  A H_____ a n_____ d_____!

4 A Are you on business?
  B No, we aren't. We're t_____. We're on holiday.

Go online for more practice

2B That's my bus!

> My cell phone is my best friend.
> Carrie Underwood, American musician

G Wh- and How questions with be **V** numbers 11–100, phone numbers **P** understanding numbers

1 GRAMMAR Wh- and How questions with be

a Complete the questions with a question word and *are* or *'s*.

1. A *Who's* Sarah Lawson?
   B She's my English teacher.

2. A _____ the concert?
   B It's on Monday.

3. A _____ she from?
   B She's from Spain.

4. A _____ your phone number?
   B It's 01279 5529284.

5. A _____ you from?
   B I'm from Brazil.

6. A _____ Mari and Laura?
   B They're on holiday in Boston.

7. A _____ Pedro?
   B He's 27.

8. A _____ your address?
   B It's 47 Bank Street.

9. A _____ you?
   B I'm fine, thanks. And you?

b Complete the conversation. Write the questions.

A [1] *What's your name* ?
B My name's Brian Halley.
A [2] _____?
B H-A-L-L-E-Y.
A Thank you. [3] _____?
B I'm from the United States.
A [4] _____?
B It's 64 Bond Street, New York City.
A Thank you. [5] _____?
B My phone number is 784-2913.
A [6] _____?
B It's b.halley@gomail.com.
A Thank you. [7] _____?
B I'm 23.
A [8] _____?
B No, I'm not. I'm single.

c Answer the questions about you.

1. What's your phone number?
   _____
2. What's your postcode?
   _____
3. Are you single?
   _____
4. What's your surname?
   _____
5. What's your address?
   _____
6. How old are you?
   _____
7. What's your email?
   _____
8. How do you spell your surname?
   _____

2 VOCABULARY numbers 11–100, phone numbers

a Complete the numbers.

1. **20** — t _w_ _e_ nt _y_
2. **15** — f _ _ t _ _ n
3. **90** — ni _ _ t _
4. **70** — s _ v _ nt _
5. **12** — t _ _ lv _
6. **100** — a hu _ _ r _ _
7. **80** — ei _ _ t _
8. **11** — e _ _ v _ _
9. **40** — fo _ t _
10. **13** — th _ r _ _ _ n
11. **60** — si _ t _

b Write the numbers.

1. forty-seven — _47_
2. nineteen — ____
3. thirty-eight — ____
4. fifty-nine — ____
5. seventy-two — ____
6. fourteen — ____
7. ninety-one — ____
8. sixteen — ____
9. twenty-three — ____
10. eighteen — ____

3 PRONUNCIATION understanding numbers

a ⏵ 2.3 Listen and complete the phone numbers.
1 0 __ 2 __ 7 __ 4 __ 3
2 __ 17 __ 9 __ 21
3 0 __ __ 35 __ 8 __ 1

b ⏵ 2.3 Listen again and repeat the phone numbers.

c ⏵ 2.4 Listen and write the numbers.
1 _17_ London Road
2 I'm ____.
3 anne.davis____@gmail.com
4 You're in room ____.
5 SW____ 4RJ

d ⏵ 2.4 Listen again and repeat the numbers.

4 WORDS AND PHRASES TO LEARN

Complete the missing words in the conversations.

1 A Wh_o's_____ sh_e_____?
   B Jenny.
   A H_____ o_____ is she?
   B She's 21.
   A W_____ c_____ is she in?
   B She's in my class.
   A She's very g_____-l_____.

2 A Hi, Tom. H_____ a_____ y_____?
   B I'm f_____, thanks.
   A Th_____ is Jenny.
   B Nice to meet you.
   C Nice to meet you, too. That's my bus. S_____ y_____ l_____.

3 A Where are you from?
   B Bournemouth.
   A Where's Bournemouth?
   B It's i_____ t_____ s_____ of England.

3A Where are my keys?

Own only what you can carry with you.
Aleksandr Solzhenitsyn, Russian writer

G singular and plural nouns, *a / an* **V** small things **P** /z/ and /s/, plural endings

1 VOCABULARY small things

Complete the crossword.

DOWN ↓

ACROSS →

2 GRAMMAR singular and plural nouns, *a / an*

a Write *a* or *an*.

1. <u>a</u> camera
2. <u>an</u> umbrella
3. ____ book
4. ____ watch
5. ____ email
6. ____ country
7. ____ city
8. ____ key
9. ____ address
10. ____ laptop
11. ____ debit card

b Write the plurals of the words in **a**.

1. <u>cameras</u>
2. _____
3. _____
4. _____
5. _____
6. _____
7. _____
8. _____
9. _____
10. _____
11. _____

c Write questions and answers.

1 <u>What is it</u>?
  <u>It's a dictionary</u>.

2 _____?
  _____.

3 _____?
  _____.

4 _____?
  _____.

5 _____?
  _____.

6 _____?
  _____.

7 _____?
  _____.

8 _____?
  _____.

d What's in your bag? Write five things.
  <u>a wallet</u>
  _____
  _____
  _____
  _____

3 PRONUNCIATION /z/ and /s/, plural endings

a 🔊 3.1 Listen and repeat the words and sounds.

zebra	1 name**s**	bag**s**
snake	2 book**s**	student**s**
/ɪz/	3 address**es**	purs**es**

b 🔊 3.2 Listen and (circle) three words with /ɪz/.

pieces   classes   coats   glasses
laptops   pencils   phones   wallets

c 🔊 3.2 Listen again and repeat the words.

4 WORDS AND PHRASES TO LEARN

Complete the conversations with a phrase from the list.

~~Oh no~~   What are they   What's in your bag
Where are my glasses

1 A Where's your bag?
  B <u>Oh no</u>! It's in the car!

2 A _____?
  B They're in your bag.

3 A Excuse me, sir. _____?
  B I have a wallet, a book, and an umbrella.

4 A _____?
  B I think they're credit cards.

Go online for more practice

3B Souvenirs

A photograph is a souvenir of life.
Deborah Smith, British translator

G this / that / these / those **V** souvenirs **P** /ð/, sentence rhythm

1 VOCABULARY souvenirs

Match the words in the list to the pictures.

~~cap~~ football shirt key ring mug
plate scarf teddy T-shirt

1 cap
2 _____ 
3 _____ 
4 _____ 
5 _____ 
6 _____  
7 _____ 
8 _____ 

2 GRAMMAR this / that / these / those

a Re-order the words to make sentences or questions.

1 these bags are
   These are bags.

2 is what that
   _____?

3 book isn't this your
   _____.

4 postcards my those are
   _____.

5 your are keys those
   _____?

6 my aren't photos these
   _____.

7 that friend is your
   _____?

8 from where this is
   _____?

b Complete the sentences with *this*, *that*, *these*, or *those*.

1 *That* 's a lovely picture!

2 **A** Is _____ a Manchester United shirt?
   B No, it's Manchester City.

3 _____ are £10.

4 A Are _____ your keys?
   B Yes, they are. Thank you!

5 Look! _____'s Martin from our English class.

6 Wow. _____ are good glasses!

7 A I like _____ cap.
   B Yes, it's very nice.

8 A Are _____ teddies £5?
   B No, they're £10.

c Complete the conversations with typical souvenirs from your country and the price.

1 A Excuse me. What are those?
  B They're <u>key rings</u>.
  A How much are they?
  B They're <u>€3.50</u>.

2 A Excuse me. What's that?
  B It's a(n) _____.
  A How much is it?
  B It's _____.

3 A Excuse me. What are these?
  B They're _____.
  A How much are they?
  B They're _____.

4 A Excuse me. What's this?
  B It's a(n) _____.
  A How much is it?
  B It's _____.

3 PRONUNCIATION /ð/ and sentence rhythm

a 🔊 3.3 Listen and complete the sentences.
   1 <u>This</u> is <u>my</u> <u>mother</u>.
   2 _____ _____ over there?
   3 _____ _____ are my keys.
   4 _____ are your _____.
   5 Is _____ your _____?

b 🔊 3.3 Listen again and repeat the sentences. <u>Copy</u> the <u>rhy</u>thm.

4 WORDS AND PHRASES TO LEARN

Complete the missing words in the conversations.

1 A H<u>ow</u> m<u>uch</u> a<u>re</u> these key rings?
  B They're €2.50.

2 A I_____ this y_____ phone?
  B Oh yes, it is. Thank you very much.
  A Y_____ w_____.

3 A Is that your bag th_____?
  B No, my bag's h_____.

4 A H_____ m_____ i_____ th_____ mug?
  B It's £5.00.

EPISODE 2 Practical English — Can I have an orange juice, please?

understanding prices, buying lunch   **P** /ʊə/, /s/, and /k/

1 UNDERSTANDING PRICES

a Write the numbers.

1 *one* cent
2 _____ dollars 
3 _____ cents 
4 _____ euros 
5 _____ pence (p) 
6 _____ pounds 

b Complete the prices.

1 €75 seventy-five *euros*
2 £21.99 twenty-one _____ ninety-nine
3 $38.50 thirty-eight _____ and fifty cents
4 40p forty _____
5 €11.60 eleven _____ sixty
6 £2.50 two _____ fifty

c Write the prices.

1 £45 *forty-five pounds*
2 £15 _____
3 €59 _____
4 99p _____
5 $1.89 _____
6 €7.25 _____
7 £4.70 _____
8 $19.85 _____

2 PRONUNCIATION /ʊə/, /s/, and /k/

a ◉ 3.4 Listen and (circle) the word with a different sound.

tourist	1 (journalist) sure European	
snake	2 pencil price coffee	
key	3 card cent camera	

b ◉ 3.4 Listen again and repeat the words.

c ◉ 3.5 Write the words in the chart. Listen and check. Then listen again and repeat the words.

~~city~~   ~~class~~   close   nice   picture   pence

snake	1 *city*
key	2 *class*

18

3 BUYING LUNCH

a Read the menu and write the prices.

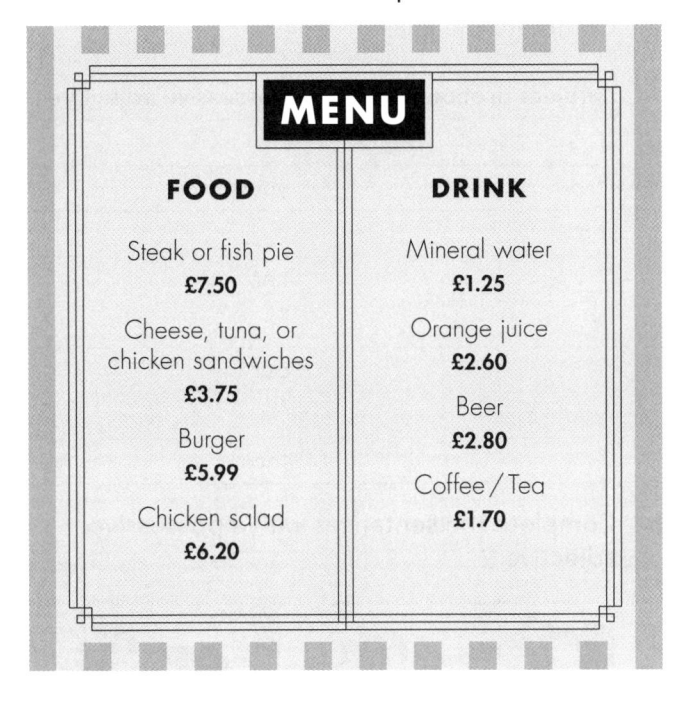

MENU

FOOD
- Steak or fish pie £7.50
- Cheese, tuna, or chicken sandwiches £3.75
- Burger £5.99
- Chicken salad £6.20

DRINK
- Mineral water £1.25
- Orange juice £2.60
- Beer £2.80
- Coffee / Tea £1.70

1 A How much is a steak pie?
  B It's _£7.50_.

2 A How much is a burger?
  B It's _____.

3 A How much is a chicken salad?
  B It's _____.

4 A How much is an orange juice?
  B It's _____.

5 A How much is a coffee?
  B It's _____.

b Complete the conversations.

a ~~Hi, yes. A chicken salad and a Diet Coke, please.~~
b Here you are.
c How much is it?
d Thanks.
e Can I have a burger and a beer, please?
f Here's your change.
g Yes, a mineral water.
h No, thanks.
i Anything else?

1
Barman Who's next?
Sally ¹_Hi. A chicken salad and a Diet Coke, please._
Barman Anything else?
Sally ² _____
Barman Ice and lemon with your drinks?
Sally ³ _____
Barman There you go. That's £7.65.
Sally ⁴ _____
Barman Thanks. Here's your change.
Sally ⁵ _____

2
Assistant Can I help you?
Dan Yes. ⁶ _____
Assistant Of course. ⁷ _____
Dan No, thanks.
Assistant There you go.
Dan Thanks. ⁸ _____
Assistant $9.25.
Dan Here you are.
Assistant Thanks. ⁹ _____
Dan Thank you. Have a nice day.

4 USEFUL PHRASES

Complete the missing words and phrases in the conversations.

1 A Seb! Hi, how are you?
  B I'm f_ine_____, th_anks_____.

2 A That's $12.75, please.
  B Here you are.
  A Thanks. H_____ your ch_____.

3 A C_____ I h_____ a cheese sandwich, please?
  B Yes, of course. Anything else?

4 A H_____ m_____ is it?
  B €8.70.

5 A We can have lunch together at the pub.
  B Sure! Gr_____ i_____.

6 A A_____ e_____?
  B And a tea, please.

4A Meet the family

> Happiness is having a large, loving family, … in another city.
> *George Burns, American comedian*

G possessive adjectives, possessive 's **V** people and family **P** /ʌ/, /æ/, and /ə/

1 VOCABULARY people and family

a Complete the chart.

singular	plural
boy	¹*boys*
²	girls
woman	³
man	⁴
⁵	friends
child	⁶
person	⁷

b Complete the sentences.

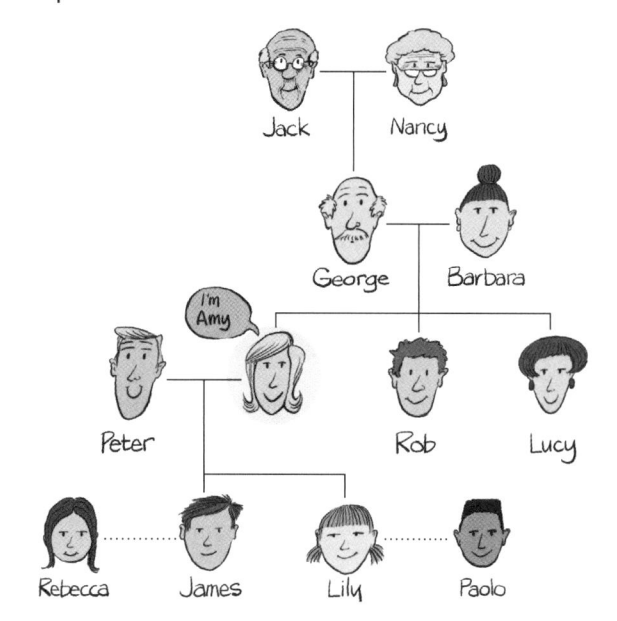

1 I'm Amy. I'm Peter's w*ife*_____.
2 George is my f_____.
3 Peter's my h_____.
4 Barbara's my m_____.
5 George and Barbara are my p_____.
6 Lily's my d_____.
7 Rob's my br_____.
8 James is my s_____.
9 Rebecca is James's g_____.
10 Lucy's my s_____.
11 Paolo is Lily's b_____.
12 Jack is my gr_____.
13 Nancy is my gr_____.
14 Jack and Nancy are my gr_____.

2 GRAMMAR possessive adjectives, possessive 's

a Complete the chart.

subject pronoun	possessive adjective
I	¹*my*
²*you*	your
he	³
⁴	her
it	⁵
⁶	our
you	⁷
⁸	their

b Complete the sentences with a possessive adjective.

1 That's *my* laptop!
2 This is _____ daughter. 
3 What's _____ name? 
4 Look at _____ coat. 
5 Here's _____ coffee, sir. 
6 This is _____ new house. 
7 It's an Italian restaurant. _____ name is Luigi's. 
8 _____ names are Emily and Joel.

c Complete the sentences.
   1 Carmen is Diego's sister.
      Diego is *Carmen's brother*.
   2 Charlotte is Peter's wife.
      Peter is _____.
   3 Mark is Angelina's brother.
      Angelina is _____.
   4 Richard is Maria's father.
      Maria is _____.
   5 Ana is Paulo's mother.
      Paulo is _____.
   6 William is Megan's husband.
      Megan is _____.
   7 Sarah is Michael's daughter.
      Michael is _____.
   8 Roberto is Luisa's son.
      Luisa is _____.

d Look at the 's in the sentences. Tick (✓) Possessive or *is*.

	Possessive	*is*
1 Mark's wife is Brazilian.	✓	
2 Angela's on holiday.		✓
3 Those are Amy's cats.		
4 It's a great phone.		
5 This is my brother's room.		
6 Jennifer's in Paris.		
7 What's your name?		
8 Peter's son is twelve.		

e Think of five people. Who are they? Write a sentence about them.
   Anna's my sister.
   Ali's my friend's brother.
   1 _____
   2 _____
   3 _____
   4 _____
   5 _____

3 **PRONUNCIATION** /ʌ/, /æ/, and /ə/

a 4.1 Listen and circle the word with a different sound.

up	1 br**o**ther M**o**nday (ph**o**ne) S**u**nday
up	2 s**o**n Th**u**rsday h**u**sband m**o**ther
cat	3 f**a**mily n**a**me th**a**nks s**a**ndwich
comput**er**	4 m**e**n fath**er** childr**e**n wom**a**n

b 4.1 Listen again and repeat the words.

4 **WORDS AND PHRASES TO LEARN**

   Complete the conversations with a phrase from the list.

   Be good   ~~Come in~~   in my phone   Let's order pizza
   on the table   What a lovely card

   1 A Hello, Billy! *Come in*_____.
      B Thank you.

   2 A Where's your phone?
      B It's _____.

   3 A What's Alice's number?
      B Just a minute. It's _____.

   4 A Frank, this is Ella. She's your babysitter today. _____.
      B OK, Mum.

   5 A _____.
      B Good idea. I love pizza.

   6 A _____!
      B It's from my sister.

4B The perfect car

I couldn't find the car of my dreams, so I built it myself.
Ferdinand Porsche, Austrian engineer

G adjectives **V** colours and common adjectives **P** /ɑː/ and /ɔː/, linking

1 VOCABULARY colours and common adjectives

a Complete the sentences with a colour.
1 E L U B
   My car is *blue*.
2 C A B L K
   Her umbrella is _____.
3 N O W B R
   His bag is _____.
4 D E R
   Gabriel's T-shirt is _____.
5 H E T I W
   The board is _____.
6 N E R G E
   Their house is _____.
7 W E Y L O L
   Amelia's coat is _____.
8 O G N R E A
   His cap is _____.

b Complete the sentences with the opposite of the **bold** word.
1 Our house isn't **small**.
   It's *big*.
2 My car isn't **fast**.
   It's _____.
3 Yulia's phone isn't **cheap**.
   It's _____.
4 His laptop isn't **new**.
   It's _____.
5 Tim's name isn't **long**.
   It's _____.
6 Their teacher isn't **bad**.
   She's _____.
7 My car isn't **clean**.
   It's _____.
8 My cat isn't **ugly**.
   It's _____.
9 This exercise isn't **easy**.
   It's _____.

c Complete the words.

1 That house is very o*ld*!
2 Is this bag e_____? 
3 This book is very l_____. 
4 The English test is d_____. 
5 Tom's sister is b_____. 
6 Those phones are ch_____.

2 GRAMMAR adjectives

a Re-order the words to make sentences.

1 I a car have blue
 I have a blue car.

2 a it's expensive camera very
 _____.

3 good they're children very
 _____.

4 a cheap that's phone
 _____.

5 has a my house red door
 _____.

6 a day it's beautiful
 _____.

7 a new tablet I have
 _____.

8 watch this nice is a
 _____.

b Rewrite the sentences.

1 The car is very slow.
 It's a *very slow car*.

2 These exercises are very easy.
 They're _____.

3 This film is very long.
 It's a _____.

4 The windows are green.
 They're _____.

5 Those umbrellas are very big.
 They're _____.

6 That phone is old.
 It's an _____.

7 The people are nice.
 They're _____.

8 The dictionary is Spanish.
 It's a _____.

3 PRONUNCIATION /ɑː/ and /ɔː/, linking

a 4.2 Listen and circle the word with a different sound.

car	1 f**a**st	(fl**a**g) f**a**ther
h**or**se	2 **o**ld	sh**or**t sm**a**ll
car	3 p**a**ssport	f**a**mily gl**a**sses
h**or**se	4 br**ow**n	t**a**ll d**augh**ter

b 4.2 Listen again and repeat the words.

c 4.3 Listen and write the phrases.
1 _____
2 _____
3 _____
4 _____
5 _____

d 4.3 Listen again and repeat the phrases.

4 WORDS AND PHRASES TO LEARN

Complete the conversation with phrases from the list.

Come with me   easy to park   I love it
in my opinion   I prefer this red car   ~~Is the car for you~~

A ¹*Is the car for you*?
B No, it's for my daughter.
C Yes, it's for me. It's my birthday.
A What about this green car here? It's small and it's ²_____.
B Well, ³_____, it's perfect for you.
C But I don't like green. ⁴_____.
B The red one? That's a sports car!
C Yes, but it's my birthday and ⁵_____!
 It's a beautiful car. How much is it?
A ⁶_____, madam.

5A A big breakfast?

> Eat breakfast like a king, lunch like a prince, and dinner like a poor man.
> *an old saying / Anonymous*

G present simple + and –: *I, you, we, they* **V** food and drink **P** word stress, /dʒ/ and /g/

1 VOCABULARY food and drink

a Complete the crossword.

DOWN ↓

ACROSS →

b What do they have for dinner? Complete the words.

1 f_i_ _s_ _h_
2 s_a_ _l_ _a_ _d_
3 t _ a

4 p _ _ _ _ a
5 v _ _ _ _ _ _ _ _ _ s
6 m _ _ k

7 m _ _ t
8 p _ _ _ _ _ _ _ s
9 w _ _ _ r

10 a s _ _ _ _ _ _ _ h
11 ch _ _ _ _ _ _ _ e
12 or _ _ _ _ e j _ _ _ _ e

2 PRONUNCIATION /dʒ/, and /g/

a ◉ 5.1 Listen and under<u>line</u> the stressed syllable.

<u>cer</u>|e|al   po|ta|toes   vege|ta|bles   cho|co|late
break|fast   sand|wich   yo|gurt

b ◉ 5.1 Listen again and repeat the words.

c ◉ 5.2 Listen and circle the word with a different sound.

/dʒ/ jazz	1 **g**et oran**ge** **j**uice
/g/ **g**irl	2 e**gg**s **J**apan su**g**ar
/dʒ/ jazz	3 sausa**ges** **g**reen ve**ge**tables
/g/ **g**irl	4 **g**ood yo**g**urt **G**ermany

d ◉ 5.2 Listen again and repeat the words.

3 GRAMMAR present simple + and –: I, you, we, they

a Complete the sentences with the + or – of the verb in brackets.

1 My friends <u>don't eat</u> healthy food. (– eat)
2 I _____ breakfast at home. (– have)
3 You _____ a lot of water. (+ drink)
4 I _____ fish. (+ like)
5 I _____ coffee in the afternoon. (– drink)
6 We _____ a salad for lunch. (+ have)
7 I don't drink tea because I _____ it. (– like)
8 My children _____ a lot of fruit. (+ eat)

b Complete the texts with the correct form of the verbs from the list.

drink   ~~have~~   not have   not like

I'm Amelie, and I'm from France. During the week, I ¹<u>have</u> breakfast in a café. I ² _____ a big breakfast, just a croissant. I ³ _____ hot chocolate. I ⁴ _____ tea or coffee.

eat   not drink   not have

My name is Laszlo and I'm from Hungary. I ⁵ _____ breakfast with my family during the week, but at weekends we sit down together. We ⁶ _____ a very big breakfast: eggs, cheese, meat, and bread. I ⁷ _____ coffee, so I have tea.

c What's your favourite meal of the day? Where do you have it? What food and drink do you have?

<u>My favourite meal of the day is</u> _____

4 WORDS AND PHRASES TO LEARN

Complete the missing words in the sentences.

1 I don't eat breakfast because I'm not h<u>ungry</u> in the morning.
2 Some doctors and scientists think breakfast is an i_____ meal.
3 Breakfast is my f_____ meal.
4 I have lunch e_____ – at 12.00.
5 I sometimes have breakfast i_____ a c_____.
6 Rice, fruit, and miso soup is a tr_____ breakfast in Japan.
7 I usually have breakfast a_____ h_____.

5B A very long flight

> I hate flying. Why? Because no one really understands how planes actually work.
> Adam Levine, American musician and actor

G present simple ?: *I, you, we, they* **V** common verb phrases 1 **P** /w/ and /v/, sentence rhythm and linking

1 GRAMMAR present simple ?: *I, you, we, they*

a Complete the interview with the questions.

Are you married?   What airline do you work for?
Do you have children?   ~~What's your name?~~
Do you like your job?   Where are you from?

Interview with a flight attendant

1 *What's your name?*
My name's Lucas.

2 _____
I'm from Rio de Janeiro. It's a big, beautiful city.

3 _____
Yes, I am. My wife's Italian. Her name is Celia.

4 _____
Yes, we do. We have a little girl. Her name's Bianca. She's three.

5 _____
I work for Gol, the Brazilian airline.

6 _____
Yes, I do. I work with my friends, and I speak to a lot of new people every day. It's very interesting.

b Complete the questions.

1 A We don't live in a flat.
   B *Do you live* in a house?

2 A I don't want a newspaper.
   B _____ a magazine?

3 A They don't like dogs.
   B _____ cats?

4 A I don't have a camera.
   B _____ a phone?

5 A I don't drink tea.
   B _____ coffee?

6 A We don't have breakfast.
   B _____ lunch?

7 A I don't need a new phone.
   B _____ tablet?

c Complete the conversation with *do* or *don't*.

Jon   ¹*Do* you have a car, Rachel?
Rachel   No, I ² _____.
Jon   Oh. ³ _____ you work in London?
Rachel   Yes, I ⁴ _____. I work in a bank.
Waiter   Excuse me. ⁵ _____ you want a coffee, sir?
Jon   Yes, please.
Waiter   And you, madam?
Rachel   No, thanks. I ⁶ _____ like coffee.
Jon   They have tea. ⁷ _____ you like tea?
Rachel   Yes, I ⁸ _____.
Waiter   OK. One coffee and one tea.

d Answer the questions about you.
1 Do you work or study?
_____
2 Where do you work / study?
_____
3 Do you have a car?
_____
4 Do you like coffee?
_____

2 VOCABULARY common verb phrases 1

Write the verbs.

| drink | eat | go | ~~have~~ | have | listen | like | live |
| need | read | speak | study | want | watch | work | |

1 _have_ lunch
2 _____ cats 
3 _____ milk 
4 _____ Chinese 
5 _____ Mexican food 
6 _____ magazines 
7 _____ a new car 
8 _____ to Brazilian music 
9 _____ in a bank 
10 _____ in a house 
11 _____ TV in the evening 
12 _____ three dogs 
13 _____ German 
14 _____ to English classes 
15 _____ a coffee 

3 PRONUNCIATION /w/ and /v/, sentence rhythm and linking

a ◎ 5.3 Listen and write the words in the correct column.

 **w**itch	 **v**ase

b ◎ 5.3 Listen again and repeat the words.

c ◎ 5.4 Listen and complete the sentences.
1 Do you _want_ a _____ sandwich?
2 I _____ _____ brother and _____ _____ teacher.
3 I _____ _____ _____ house _____ _____ small city.
4 I _____ _____ _____ _____ TV.

d ◎ 5.4 Listen again and repeat the sentences. Copy the rhythm.

4 WORDS AND PHRASES TO LEARN

Complete the conversations with a phrase from the list.

~~Can I see your passport and boarding pass, please~~   Do you want fish or pasta
keep the change   What time do we arrive

1 A _Can I see your passport and boarding pass, please?_
  B Yes, here you are.

2 A Excuse me, madam. _____?
  B Fish, please.

3 A _____?
  B In 15 minutes, sir.

4 A That's £4.75, please.
  B Here you are – _____.

Go online for more practice   27

EPISODE 3 Practical English What time is it?

telling the time V the time, saying how you feel P /ɒ/, silent consonants

1 TELLING THE TIME

Complete the conversations.

1 A What _time_ is it?
   B It's _quarter_ to eleven.

2 A It's ten to five. What _____ your train?
   B _____ five fifteen.

3 A What time is _____?
   B It's quarter _____ four.

4 A Hello. I'm _____ I'm late.
   B You're two hours late – _____ 11.30!

2 VOCABULARY the time

a Complete the times.

1 It's _half_ past two.
2 It's eight _____. 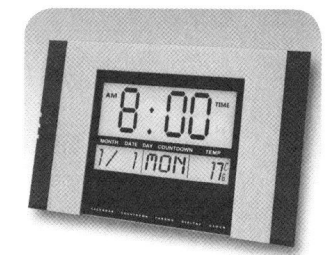
3 It's _____ past ten. 
4 It's a _____ to six. 
5 It's _____ past eleven. 
6 It's _____ to one. 
7 It's _____ past nine. 
8 It's _____ to seven. 
9 It's _____ past five. 
10 It's _____ to twelve. 
11 It's _____ past three. 
12 It's _____ to four. 

b ◉ 5.5 Listen and draw the times on the clocks.

1 2 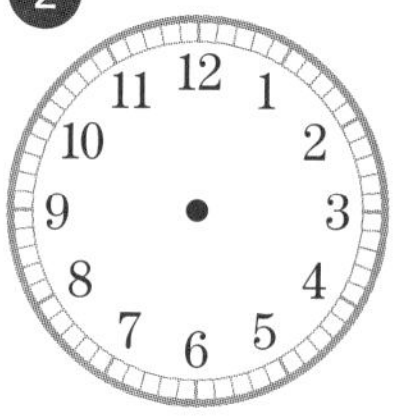 3 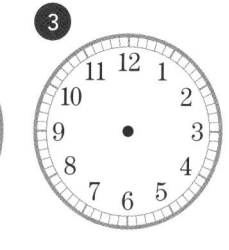 4  5 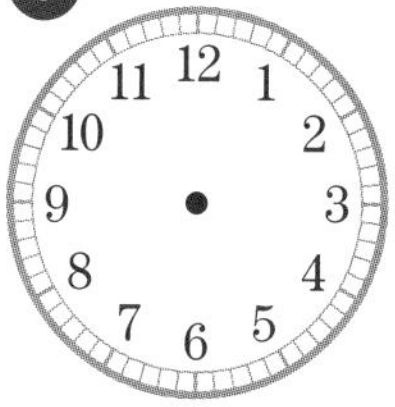 6

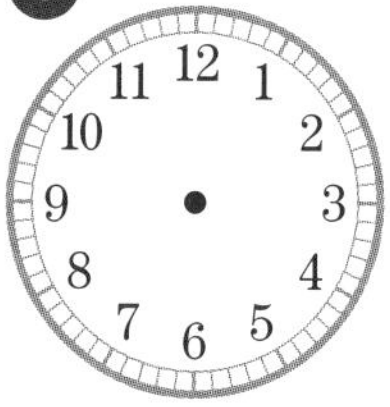

3 PRONUNCIATION /ɒ/, silent consonants

a 🔊 5.6 Listen and circle the word with a different sound.

1	wh**a**t	(sm**all**)	h**o**t
2	m**o**ther	s**o**rry	n**o**t
3	**O**xford	c**o**ffee	s**o**n
4	w**a**tch	**o**ld	**o**range
5	l**o**ng	w**a**nt	n**o**w

b 🔊 5.6 Listen again and repeat the words.

c 🔊 5.7 Listen and cross out the silent consonants in these words.

1 half
2 hour
3 know
4 listen
5 two
6 Wednesday
7 what
8 write

d 🔊 5.7 Listen again and repeat the words.

4 VOCABULARY saying how you feel

Complete the sentences.

1 He's _hot_.

2 He's _____.

3 She's _____.

4 She's _____.

5 He's _____.

5 USEFUL PHRASES

Complete the missing words and phrases in the conversation.

A Hi, Adam. I'm ¹<u>really</u> s<u>orry</u> I'm late. What time's the film?
B ²D_____ w_____. It's OK – it's at half past seven. It's only ten past seven.

* * *

A ³W_____ a gr_____ film!
B Yes – fantastic! Do you want to go to the pub now?
A But it's half past ten. It's ⁴l_____ and I'm ⁵t_____.
B ⁶C_____ o_____. I know a really good pub near here.
A Oh, OK. ⁷L_____ g_____.

6A A school reunion

> Find a job you like and you add five days to every week.
> H. Jackson Brown, Jr., American author

G present simple: *he, she, it* **V** jobs and places of work **P** third person -es, sentence rhythm

1 GRAMMAR present simple: *he, she, it*

a Look at the chart and complete the sentences.

	Amy	Luis
live in a big city	✗	✓
like cats	✓	✗
listen to pop music	✓	✗
speak French	✗	✓
drink tea	✗	✓

1 Amy *doesn't live* in a big city.
2 She _____ cats.
3 She _____ to pop music.
4 She _____ French.
5 She _____ tea.
6 Luis _____ in a big city.
7 He _____ cats.
8 He _____ to pop music.
9 He _____ French.
10 He _____ tea.

b Complete the text with the correct form of the verbs in brackets.

Kate's from Ireland, and she's an English teacher in Russia. She ¹*lives* (live) in St Petersburg, and she ² _____ (work) in a language school in the centre of the city. She ³ _____ (not work) at the weekends because the school is closed. Kate ⁴ _____ (like) Russia, but she ⁵ _____ (not speak) Russian very well. She ⁶ _____ (have) a Russian class in the morning, and she ⁷ _____ (study) in the evening on her computer. She ⁸ _____ (watch) TV at home, but she ⁹ _____ (not understand) very much. She ¹⁰ _____ (think) Russia is a fantastic country, and she ¹¹ _____ (not want) to go home.

c Complete the conversation with *do, does, don't,* or *doesn't*.

Mike Hello, I'm Mike.
Sarah Hi, I'm Sarah.
Mike What ¹*do* you do, Sarah?
Sarah I'm a journalist.
Mike ² _____ you work for a newspaper?
Sarah No, I ³ _____ . I work for a magazine.
Mike Where ⁴ _____ you work?
Sarah I work in different places. At home, in the office, in the street…
Mike ⁵ _____ you like your job?
Sarah Yes, I ⁶ _____ . It's really interesting.
Mike Where ⁷ _____ you live?
Sarah I have a very small flat in the centre of the city.
Mike ⁸ _____ you have brothers and sisters?
Sarah Yes, I have one brother.
Mike What ⁹ _____ he do?
Sarah He works in a shop.
Mike ¹⁰ _____ he have a flat?
Sarah No, he ¹¹ _____ . He lives with our parents.

d Think of a friend or a member of your family and complete the sentences.

1 He / She lives in _____ .
2 He / She likes _____ .
3 He / She watches _____ .
4 He / She drinks _____ .
5 He / She has _____ .

2 PRONUNCIATION third person -es

a ◆)) 6.1 Listen and (circle) four more words with /ɪz/ and write them in the chart.

(closes) does eats finishes has goes likes
listens lives loves reads relaxes speaks
teaches wants watches works

/ɪz/	closes

b ◆)) 6.1 Listen again and repeat the words.

30

3 VOCABULARY jobs and places of work

a Complete the puzzle. What's the mystery word?

[Crossword puzzle with answer row: R E _ _ _ _ _ _ _ _ S T, with down clues: ¹TEACHER, ²D, ³N, ⁴S, ⁵F, ⁶T, ⁷P, ⁸J, ⁹W]

b Complete the sentences.

1 A factory worker works in a f<u>actory</u>.
2 A writer works at h_____.
3 A teacher works in a sc_____.
4 A waitress works in a r_____.
5 A policeman works in the st_____.
6 A nurse works in a h_____.
7 A shop assistant works in a sh_____.
8 A receptionist works in a hotel or an o_____.

4 PRONUNCIATION sentence rhythm

a 6.2 Listen and complete the conversations.

1 A What <u>does</u> <u>she</u> do?
　B _____ _____ journalist.
　A _____ _____ like her job?
　B Yes, _____ _____.

2 A What _____ _____ do?
　B _____ _____ waiter.
　A Where _____ _____ work?
　B _____ _____ café.

b 6.2 Listen again and repeat the sentences. Copy the rhythm.

5 WORDS AND PHRASES TO LEARN

Complete the conversations with a word or phrase from the list.

Because   Great to see you.
He's married to Lisa   How awful
I love your shoes   What does she do

1 A Who's that man with grey hair?
　B That's Simon. <u>He's married to Lisa</u>.

2 A Lisa, Karl, hi! _____.
　B Hello, Max. You too.

3 A _____ – they're beautiful!
　B Thank you – they're new.

4 A _____?
　B She's a nurse.

5 A Poor Diane isn't very well. She's in hospital.
　B Oh no! _____!

6 A Why do you get up at 5.30?
　B _____ I start work at 6.30.

Go online for more practice   31

6B Good morning, goodnight

> Think in the morning. Act in the afternoon. Eat in the evening. Sleep at night.
> *William Blake, British poet and artist*

G adverbs of frequency **V** a typical day **P** /j/ and /juː/, sentence rhythm

1 VOCABULARY a typical day

a Complete the verb phrases.

1 g*et* up
2 f_____ work 
3 g_____ shopping 
4 h_____ a shower 
5 d_____ housework 
6 m_____ dinner 
7 w_____ TV 
8 g_____ to bed 

b Write the words in the chart.

~~a bath~~   a coffee   breakfast   dinner   ~~home~~
lunch   to bed   to school   to the gym   to work

have	go
a bath	home

c Complete the text with the correct verbs.

do   ~~finish~~   get up   go (x4)   have (x3)   watch

I'm Hannah, and I'm a nurse. I work at night and I sleep during the day. I ¹*finish* work at eight o'clock in the morning, and then I ²_____ home and I ³_____ to bed. I ⁴_____ at about four o'clock in the afternoon, and I ⁵_____ some cereal and orange juice for breakfast. Then I ⁶_____ shopping and I ⁷_____ the housework or ⁸_____ TV. At seven o'clock in the evening I ⁹_____ a shower, and I ¹⁰_____ dinner before I ¹¹_____ to work again.

2 PRONUNCIATION /j/ and /juː/, sentence rhythm

a 🔊 6.3 Listen and tick (✓) the words which have the /j/ sound.

1 yellow ✓
2 factory ✗
3 young
4 yogurt
5 ugly
6 easy
7 boy
8 your
9 grey
10 yes

b 🔊 6.3 Listen again and repeat the words.

c 🔊 6.4 Listen and tick (✓) the words which have the /juː/ sound.

1 usually ✓
2 umbrella ✗
3 study
4 student
5 music
6 number
7 beautiful
8 juice
9 newspaper
10 hurry

d 🔊 6.4 Listen again and repeat the words.

e 🔊 **6.5 Listen and complete the sentences.**
1 I start work _at_ nine _in_ _the_ morning.
2 She _____ _____ coffee _____ _____ quarter _____ ten.
3 They _____ _____ sandwich _____ _____ café.
4 _____ finish work _____ six thirty.
5 _____ _____ housework _____ _____ weekend.
6 _____ watches TV _____ _____ evening.

f 🔊 **6.5 Listen again and repeat. Copy the rhythm.**

3 GRAMMAR adverbs of frequency

a Rewrite the sentences. Use the words in brackets.
1 I get up early. (always)
   I always get up early.
2 Yasmin goes to school by bus. (usually)
   _____.
3 You do housework. (never)
   _____.
4 They have fish for dinner. (sometimes)
   _____.
5 Andy has lunch at home. (always)
   _____.
6 I watch TV in the morning. (never)
   _____.
7 We go shopping at the weekend. (sometimes)
   _____.
8 They have coffee for breakfast. (usually)
   _____.

b Look at the chart and complete the sentences.

✓✓✓✓✓ = always
✓✓✓ = usually
✓ = sometimes
✗ = never

	Diego	Jen
go to the gym	✗	✓✓✓✓
read magazines	✓	✓✓✓
watch football on TV	✓✓✓✓✓	✓
get up early	✓✓✓	✗

1 Diego _never goes_ to the gym.
2 He _____ magazines.
3 He _____ football on TV.
4 He _____ early.
5 Jen _____ to the gym.
6 She _____ magazines.
7 She _____ football on TV.
8 She _____ early.

c Write about your typical evening. Use adverbs of frequency.
I always make dinner for my family. We usually eat at 7.00.
_____
_____
_____
_____
_____

4 WORDS AND PHRASES TO LEARN

Complete the conversations with a word or phrase from the list.

~~Are you a morning person~~   every morning   feel tired
He gets up about 8.00   on the way to work
What time do you get up

1 A _Are you a morning person?_
   B Yes, I get up at 6.00 every day.
2 A _____?
   B I usually get up about 9.30. I don't get up early.
3 A What time does Harry get up?
   B _____.
4 A What do you do _____?
   B I usually read a magazine on the bus.
5 A What do you have for breakfast?
   B I have cereal and orange juice _____.
6 A Why do you go to bed at 8.30? It's very early.
   B Because I always _____ after work.

ANSWER KEY

1A

1 GRAMMAR

a 3 I'm not Helen.
   4 You aren't a teacher.
   5 I'm Rob.
   6 You're in my class.
   7 I'm in room 4.
   8 You aren't Diana.

b 3 I'm not Jenny.
   4 I'm not in class 2.
   5 Am I in room 4?
   6 Are you Dom?
   7 I'm not a student.
   8 Are you in class 7?

c 2 Are you, I am
   3 I'm, I'm
   4 I'm, I'm not
   5 Are you, I am
   6 I'm, I'm
   7 Am I, you aren't
   8 Are you, I am

2 VOCABULARY

a nine, one, three, two, eight, six, seven, zero, five

b 1 one
   2 two
   3 three
   4 four
   5 five
   6 six
   7 seven
   8 eight
   9 nine
   10 ten

c 2 Wednesday
   3 Saturday
   4 Tuesday
   5 Sunday
   6 Thursday
   7 Friday

d Students' own answers.

3 PRONUNCIATION

a /h/ Helen, hello
   /aɪ/ nice
   /iː/ meet, tea

4 WORDS AND PHRASES TO LEARN

2 Nice to meet you
3 What's your name
4 See you tomorrow
5 Sorry
6 Thanks

1B

1 VOCABULARY

a Across: 5 Brazil, 6 Japan
   Down: 2 England, 3 China, 4 Spain

b 2 France
   3 Italy
   4 the United States
   5 Russia
   6 Turkey
   7 Poland
   8 Egypt
   9 Germany

2 GRAMMAR

a 3 She's
   4 He's
   5 It's
   6 She's
   7 He's
   8 It's

b 1 's
   2 's, Is, is
   3 Is, isn't, 's
   4 Is, isn't, 's

c 3 Is Salma Hayek from Mexico?
     Yes, she is. She's from Veracruz.
   4 Is Naples in Turkey?
     No, it isn't. It's in Italy.
   5 Is Copacabana in Brazil?
     Yes, it is. It's in Rio.
   6 Is Lublin in Russia?
     No, it isn't. It's in Poland.
   7 Is Gary Oldman from England?
     Yes, he is. He's from London.
   8 Is Geneva in France?
     No, it isn't. It's in Switzerland.
   9 Is Javier Bardem from Spain?
     Yes, he is. He's from Las Palmas.
   10 Is the Louvre in Italy?
     No, it isn't. It's in France.

d Students' own answers.

3 PRONUNCIATION

a 2 two, 3 classroom, 4 Spain

4 WORDS AND PHRASES TO LEARN

1 It's a nice city
2 I think she's from Spain
3 I don't know
4 Where's Basel

Practical English

1 THE ALPHABET

a 2 E
   3 G
   4 H
   5 C
   6 Y
   7 O
   8 T

f 1 /iː/ please, she, teacher
   2 /e/ help, spell
   3 /eɪ/ name, Spain, table

2 VOCABULARY

a 2 laptop
   3 pen
   4 table
   5 door
   6 chair
   7 window
   8 dictionary
   9 bag
   10 coat
   11 piece, paper

b 2 repeat
   3 Look
   4 Open
   5 understand
   6 spell
   7 Go
   8 books
   9 Stand
   10 Sit
   11 Excuse
   12 late

3 CHECKING INTO A HOTEL

2 reservation
3 name
4 spell
5 surname
6 room

4 BOOKING A TABLE

2 e, 3 d, 4 a, 5 c

5 USEFUL PHRASES

2 I have a reservation
3 How do you spell it
4 That's right
5 Good morning
6 A table for tomorrow, please
7 Sorry
8 Thank you

2A

1 VOCABULARY

2 Japanese
3 British
4 Brazilian
5 Polish
6 Chinese
7 Russian
8 English
9 Mexican
10 Egyptian
11 Turkish
12 American
13 Swiss

The mystery word is 'nationalities'.

2 PRONUNCIATION

a /dʒ/ German, Japanese, just
   /tʃ/ French, teacher
   /ʃ/ Egyptian, Russian, Turkish

ANSWER KEY

3 GRAMMAR

a 2 You're teachers. You aren't students.
   3 They're Chinese. They aren't Japanese.
   4 We're from Mexico. We aren't from Brazil.
   5 You're in class 3. You aren't in class 2.
   6 They're from Egypt. They aren't from Turkey.
   7 She's in room 4. She isn't in room 5.
   8 I'm Polish. I'm not Russian.

b 2 They're in class 6.
   3 She's on holiday.
   4 He's from Brazil.
   5 We're here on business.
   6 It's in Canada.

c 2 Are they in class 1
   3 Are they from England
   4 Is Fernanda Italian
   5 Is Zurich in Switzerland

d b 2, c 1, d 5, e 3

e Students' own answers.

4 WORDS AND PHRASES TO LEARN

2 Are you on holiday
3 Have a nice day
4 tourists

2B

1 GRAMMAR

a 2 When's
   3 Where's
   4 What's
   5 Where are
   6 Where are
   7 How old's
   8 What's
   9 How are

b 2 How do you spell your surname
   3 Where are you from
   4 What's your address
   5 What's your phone number
   6 What's your email address
   7 How old are you
   8 Are you married

c Students' own answers.

2 VOCABULARY

a 2 fifteen
   3 ninety
   4 seventy
   5 twelve
   6 a hundred
   7 eighty
   8 eleven
   9 forty
   10 thirteen
   11 sixty

b 2 19, 3 38, 4 59, 5 72, 6 14, 7 91, 8 16, 9 23, 10 18

3 PRONUNCIATION

a 1 9, 2, 5, 4, 0, 1, 3
   2 0, 2, 5, 6, 8, 7
   3 2, 8, 6, 9, 7

c 2 23
   3 77
   4 65
   5 12

4 WORDS AND PHRASES TO LEARN

1 How old, Whose class, good-looking
2 How are you, fine, This, See you later
3 in the south

3A

1 VOCABULARY

Down: 2 tablet, 4 passport, 6 bag, 7 wallet, 9 credit card, 10 camera, 11 notebook, 12 glasses
Across: 3 photo, 4 phone, 5 umbrella, 8 pencil, 11 newspaper, 13 charger, 14 ID card, 15 key

2 GRAMMAR

a 3 a, 4 a, 5 an, 6 a, 7 a, 8 a, 9 an, 10 a, 11 a

b 2 umbrellas
   3 books
   4 watches
   5 emails
   6 countries
   7 cities
   8 keys
   9 addresses
   10 laptops
   11 debit cards

c 2 What are they, They're keys
   3 What is it, It's a photo
   4 What are they, They're pens
   5 What is it, It's an ID card
   6 What is it, It's a door
   7 What is it, It's a table
   8 What are they, They're coats

d Students' own answers.

3 PRONUNCIATION

b pieces, classes, glasses

4 WORDS AND PHRASES TO LEARN

2 Where are my glasses
3 What's in your bag
4 What are they

3B

1 VOCABULARY

2 key ring, 3 plate, 4 teddy, 5 mug, 6 scarf, 7 T-shirt, 8 football shirt

2 GRAMMAR

a 2 What is that
   3 This isn't your book
   4 Those are my postcards
   5 Are those your keys
   6 These aren't my photos
   7 Is that your friend
   8 Where is this from

b 2 this, 3 Those, 4 these, 5 That's, 6 These, 7 that, 8 these

c Students' own answers.

3 PRONUNCIATION

a 2 that
   3 Those
   4 These, books
   5 this, phone

4 WORDS AND PHRASES TO LEARN

2 Is … your, You're welcome
3 there, here
4 How much is that / this

Practical English

1 UNDERSTANDING PRICES

a 2 one hundred
   3 twenty
   4 fifty
   5 five
   6 ten

b 2 pounds
   3 dollars
   4 pence / p
   5 euros
   6 pounds

c 2 fifteen pounds
   3 fifty-nine euros
   4 ninety-nine pence / p
   5 one dollar eighty-nine
   6 seven euros twenty-five
   7 four pounds seventy
   8 nineteen dollars eighty-five

2 PRONUNCIATION

a 2 coffee
   3 cent

c /s/ nice, pence
   /k/ close, picture

3 BUYING LUNCH

a 2 £5.99
   3 £6.20
   4 £2.60
   5 £1.70

b 2 g
   3 h
   4 b
   5 d
   6 e
   7 i
   8 c
   9 f

4 USEFUL PHRASES

2 Here's, change
3 Can, have
4 How much
5 Great idea
6 Anything else

ANSWER KEY

4A

1 VOCABULARY

a 2 girl
   3 women
   4 men
   5 friend
   6 children
   7 people

b 2 father
   3 husband
   4 mother
   5 parents
   6 daughter
   7 brother
   8 son
   9 girlfriend
   10 sister
   11 boyfriend
   12 grandfather
   13 grandmother
   14 grandparents

2 GRAMMAR

a 3 his
   4 she
   5 its
   6 we
   7 your
   8 they

b 2 our
   3 his
   4 her
   5 your
   6 our
   7 Its
   8 Their

c 2 Charlotte's husband
   3 Mark's sister
   4 Richard's daughter
   5 Ana's son
   6 William's wife
   7 Sarah's father
   8 Roberto's mother

d 3 Possessive
   4 *is*
   5 Possessive
   6 *is*
   7 *is*
   8 Possessive

e Students' own answers.

3 PRONUNCIATION

2 Thursday
3 name
4 men

4 WORDS AND PHRASES TO LEARN

2 on the table
3 in my phone
4 Be good
5 Let's order pizza
6 What a lovely card

4B

1 VOCABULARY

a 2 black
   3 brown
   4 red
   5 white
   6 green
   7 yellow
   8 orange

b 2 slow
   3 expensive
   4 old
   5 short
   6 good
   7 dirty
   8 beautiful
   9 difficult

c 2 expensive
   3 long
   4 difficult
   5 beautiful
   6 cheap

2 GRAMMAR

a 2 It's a very expensive camera
   3 They're very good children
   4 That's a cheap phone
   5 My house has a red door
   6 It's a beautiful day
   7 I have a new tablet
   8 This is a nice watch

b 2 very easy exercises
   3 very long film
   4 green windows
   5 very big umbrellas
   6 old phone
   7 nice people
   8 Spanish dictionary

3 PRONUNCIATION

a 2 old
   3 family
   4 brown

c 1 an American car
   2 a nice evening
   3 an expensive phone
   4 a long email
   5 an orange juice

4 WORDS AND PHRASES TO LEARN

2 easy to park
3 in my opinion
4 I prefer this red car
5 I love it
6 Come with me

5A

1 VOCABULARY

a Down: 1 coffee, 2 yogurt, 3 cereal, 5 sugar, 7 fruit, 10 rice
   Across: 4 eggs, 6 cheese, 8 bread, 9 butter

b 3 tea
   4 pasta
   5 vegetables
   6 milk
   7 meat
   8 potatoes
   9 water
   10 a sandwich
   11 chocolate
   12 orange juice

2 PRONUNCIATION

a po<u>ta</u>toes, <u>ve</u>getables, <u>cho</u>colate, <u>break</u>fast, <u>sand</u>wich, <u>yo</u>gurt

c 2 Japan, 3 green, 4 Germany

3 GRAMMAR

a 2 don't have
   3 drink
   4 like
   5 don't drink
   6 have
   7 don't like
   8 eat

b 2 don't have
   3 drink
   4 don't like / don't have
   5 don't like / don't have
   6 eat
   7 don't drink

c Students' own answers.

4 WORDS AND PHRASES TO LEARN

2 important
3 favourite
4 early
5 in, café
6 traditional
7 at home

5B

1 GRAMMAR

a 2 Where are you from?
   3 Are you married?
   4 Do you have children?
   5 What airline do you work for?
   6 Do you like your job?

b 2 Do you want
   3 Do they like
   4 Do you have
   5 Do you drink
   6 Do you have
   7 Do you need a new

c 2 don't
   3 Do
   4 do
   5 Do
   6 don't
   7 Do
   8 do

d Students' own answers.

ANSWER KEY

2 VOCABULARY
2 like
3 drink
4 speak
5 eat
6 read
7 need
8 listen
9 work
10 live
11 watch
12 have
13 study
14 go
15 want

3 PRONUNCIATION
a /w/: want, where, when, work
/v/: very, live, TV, have
c 2 have a, he's a
3 live in a, in a
4 watch a lot of

4 WORDS AND PHRASES TO LEARN
2 Do you want fish or pasta
3 What time do we arrive
4 keep the change

Practical English

1 TELLING THE TIME
2 time's, At
3 it, to
4 sorry, it's

2 VOCABULARY
a 2 o'clock
3 quarter
4 quarter
5 ten
6 twenty
7 twenty-five
8 five
9 five
10 ten
11 twenty
12 twenty-five

b 1, 2, 3, 4, 5, 6 (clock faces)

3 PRONUNCIATION
a 2 mother
3 son
4 old
5 now

c 2 hour
3 know
4 listen
5 two
6 Wednesday
7 what
8 write

4 VOCABULARY
2 tired
3 cold
4 thirsty
5 hungry

5 USEFUL PHRASES
2 Don't worry
3 What, great
4 late
5 tired
6 Come on
7 Let's go

6A

1 GRAMMAR
a 2 likes
3 listens
4 doesn't speak
5 doesn't drink
6 lives
7 doesn't like
8 doesn't listen
9 speaks
10 drinks

b 2 works
3 doesn't work
4 likes
5 doesn't speak
6 has
7 studies
8 watches
9 doesn't understand
10 thinks
11 doesn't want

c 2 Do
3 don't
4 do
5 Do
6 do
7 do
8 Do
9 does
10 Does
11 doesn't

d Students' own answers.

2 PRONUNCIATION
a finishes, relaxes, teaches, watches

3 VOCABULARY
a 2 doctor
3 nurse
4 shop assistant
5 factory worker
6 taxi driver
7 policewoman
8 journalist
9 waitress

The mystery word is 'receptionist'.

b 2 home
3 school
4 restaurant
5 street
6 hospital
7 shop
8 office

4 PRONUNCIATION
a 1 She's a, Does she, she does
2 does he, He's a, does he, He works in a

5 WORDS AND PHRASES TO LEARN
2 Great to see you.
3 I love your shoes
4 What does she do
5 How awful
6 Because

ANSWER KEY

6B

1 VOCABULARY

a 2 finish
   3 go
   4 have
   5 do
   6 make
   7 watch
   8 go

b have: a coffee, breakfast, dinner, lunch
   go: to bed, to school, to the gym, to work

c 2 go
   3 go
   4 get up
   5 have
   6 go
   7 do
   8 watch
   9 have
   10 have
   11 go

2 PRONUNCIATION

a 3 ✓, 4 ✓, 5 ✗, 6 ✗, 7 ✓, 8 ✓, 9 ✓, 10 ✓
c 3 ✗, 4 ✓, 5 ✓, 6 ✗, 7 ✓, 8 ✓, 9 ✓, 10 ✗
d 2 has a, at a, past
   3 have a, at a
   4 You, at
   5 We do, at the
   6 He, in the

3 GRAMMAR

a 2 Yasmin usually goes to school by bus.
   3 You never do housework.
   4 They sometimes have fish for dinner.
   5 Andy always has lunch at home.
   6 I never watch TV in the morning.
   7 We sometimes go shopping at the weekend.
   8 They usually have coffee for breakfast.

b 2 sometimes reads
   3 always watches
   4 usually gets up
   5 always goes
   6 usually reads
   7 sometimes watches
   8 never gets up

c Students' own answers.

OXFORD
UNIVERSITY PRESS

Great Clarendon Street, Oxford, OX2 6DP, United Kingdom

Oxford University Press is a department of the University of Oxford. It furthers the University's objective of excellence in research, scholarship, and education by publishing worldwide. Oxford is a registered trade mark of Oxford University Press in the UK and in certain other countries

© Oxford University Press 2019

The moral rights of the author have been asserted

First published in 2019

2023 2022 2021 2020 2019

10 9 8 7 6 5 4 3 2 1

No unauthorized photocopying

All rights reserved. No part of this publication may be reproduced, stored in a retrieval system, or transmitted, in any form or by any means, without the prior permission in writing of Oxford University Press, or as expressly permitted by law, by licence or under terms agreed with the appropriate reprographics rights organization. Enquiries concerning reproduction outside the scope of the above should be sent to the ELT Rights Department, Oxford University Press, at the address above

You must not circulate this work in any other form and you must impose this same condition on any acquirer

Links to third party websites are provided by Oxford in good faith and for information only. Oxford disclaims any responsibility for the materials contained in any third party website referenced in this work

ISBN: 978 0 19 402975 9

Printed in China

This book is printed on paper from certified and well-managed sources

ACKNOWLEDGEMENTS

Back cover photograph: Oxford University Press building/David Fisher

The authors would like to thank all the teachers and students round the world whose feedback has helped us to shape English File.

The authors would also like to thank: all those at Oxford University Press (both in Oxford and around the world) and the design team who have contributed their skills and ideas to producing this course.

Finally very special thanks from Clive to Maria Angeles, Lucia, and Eric, and from Christina to Cristina, for all their support and encouragement. Christina would also like to thank her children Joaquin, Marco, and Krysia for their constant inspiration.

Student's Book

The publisher and authors are very grateful to the following who have provided personal stories and/or photographs: Hannah Donat and Dominic Latham-Koenig.

The publisher and authors would also like to thank the following for their invaluable feedback on the materials: Magdalena Muszyńska, Brian Brennan, Krysia Mabbott, Dagmara Łata, Elif Barbaros, Zahra Bilides, Kenny McDonnell, Rosa María Iglesias Traviesas, Yolanda Calpe, Ana María Vallejo Guijarro, Patricia Ares.

Sources: www.express.co.uk; www.dailymail.co.uk/femail

Although every effort has been made to trace and contact copyright holders before publication, this has not been possible in some cases. We apologize for any apparent infringement of copyright and if notified, the publisher will be pleased to rectify any errors or omissions at the earliest opportunity.

We would also like to thank the following for permission to reproduce the following photographs: 123RF pp.18 (one umbrella/Tatiana Popova), (four pencils/Liubov Shirokova), (two laptops/zentilia), 19 (E/Hemant Mehta); Alamy pp.9 (3/richard sowersby), (5/Steve Barnett), (7/World Discovery), (11/Roger Bamber), 10 (6/Shotshop GmbH), 12 (1/Michael Willis), (2/B Christopher), (3/Richard Sharrocks), (4/Martin Lee), 19 (A/Photoinke), (12/Paul Herbert), 20 (stall/James Clarke Images), 22 (£10 GBP/Nick Fielding), (£10 Euros/Iakov Filimonov), ($10 US/Joe Sohm/Visions of America, LLC), 26 (Tizzy/Simon Stuart-Miller), 27 (films/Everett Collection Inc), 34 (smartphone inset in A/Mike Abbott), (wristwatch repeated/musk), 82 (10 Swatch/Richard Levine), 117 (3/blickwinkel), (5/JLImages), (7/AF archive), (10/View Pictures Ltd), (13/Prisma Bildagentur AG), 121 (Colours 6/Jeffrey Blackler), (Colours 8/Oleksiy Maksymenko Photography), (Adjectives 9/Jeffrey Blackler), 122 (sandwich/Barry Mason), (water/Gerhard Beneken/docstock), 123 (TV/Picture Partners), (drink tea/sebastiano volponi/MARKA), (bank/Image Source Plus), 124 (police officers/Janine Wiedel Photolibrary), (restaurant/Andrew Twort), (office/Hufton + Crow/View Pictures Ltd), (school/Art Directors & TRIP), (factory/Jim West); Hannah Donat p.38 (Hannah and Kit), 78 (10 Swatch/Richard Levine); Getty Images pp.8 (2/Onoky – Fabrice Lerouge), (Caetano Veloso/Damian Dopacio/AFP), (Lila Downs/Omar Vega/LatinContent Editorial), 9 (1/Joey Foley/Getty Images Entertainment), (2/Jupiterimages/The Image Bank), (4/Egyptian), (10/Jon Furniss/WireImage), (12/Gustavo Caballero/Getty Images Entertainment), 13 (1/Jerod Harris/Getty Images Entertainment), (4/Jim Spellman/WireImage), 16 (pen/Donald Erickson/Collection E+), 17 (Mark/NicolasMcComber/E+), 28 (wallet/Creative Crop), 29 (Jeremy Fisher and family/Philip and Karen SmithCollection/Photographer's Choice RF), (Claire and her sisters/Westend61), 30 (Sakura/Tadamasa Taniguchi), (coffee in office/Gregor Schuster), 35 (tired/Christopher Hope-Fitch), (hungry/John Lund/Marc Romanelli/Blend Images), (hot/Cultura/Chris Whitehead), (thirsty/Peter Cade/Iconica), 36 (1/Chris Condon/US PGA Tour), (3/Frederic Lucano/The Image Bank), 78 (2/Visual China Group), (3/Giuseppe Cacace/AFP), (4/Alex Davies/FilmMagic), (5/Michael Melford/National Geographic Magazines), (6/Victor Virgile/Gamma-Rapho), (7/Bloomberg), (9/Jose Perez Gegundez/Gamma-Rapho), 82 (reused from p.78), 117 (2/Luis Castaneda Inc,), (6/Izzet Keribar), 120 (People 1/Stefka Pavlova/Moment Open), (People 2/Gen Umekita), 121 (Colours 9/Nikada/E+), (Adjectives 2/Michael Melford/Photographer's Choice), (Adjectives 5/Car Culture), (Adjectives 6/Ken Ishii/Getty Images AsiaPac), 123 (radio/Frontdoor Images/Stone), (dog/Rafael Elias), (cats/Cultura/Zak Kendal), (broken down car/Rhienna Cutler/E+), 124 (journalist/Max Mumby/Indigo), (shop assistant/Bloomberg), (receptionist/Frederic Lucano/The Image Bank), (factory worker/Monty Rakusen/Cultura), (cab driver/Jupiterimages/Photolibrary), (department store/Bloomberg), (desk at home/Westend61); Christina Latham-Koenig p.37; Reproduced by permission of Oxford University Press from Oxford Essential Dictionary © Oxford University Press 2012 p.16 (dictionary); Oxford University Press pp.18 (one pencil), 22 (50 cents), 40 (bread), (orange juice), 117 (9), 120 (Family 1 & 2), (Family 7-8/Image Source/Getty Images), 121 (Adjectives 15), (Adjectives 16); Oxford University Press\Alamy pp.16 (whiteboard/RTimages), (door/Dmytro Grankin), 22 (50 pence/Images), 35 (cold/XiXinXing), 86 (family), 116 (Sean Gladwell), 117 (4/Jan Tadeusz), (8/Sean Pavone), 120 (People 6/Image Source), (Family 3-6/D. Hurst), (Family 11-12/Ojo Images Ltd), 121 (Colours 3/Marek Kosmal), (Colours 7/Nalinratana Phiyanalinmat), (Colours 10/Artem Merzlenko), (Adjectives 10/Picturebank), 122 (yoghurt/FoodFood), (milk/Valentyn Volkov), (orange juice/imageBroker), (man drinking/Mint Images), 123 (flat/UpperCut Images), (breakfast/UpperCut Images), (newspaper/Juice Images), (speak English/Andres Rodriguez), (want coffee/Image Source Plus), (polystyrene cup/Judith Collins), (classes/Cathy Topping), 124 (nurse/OJO Images Ltd), (hospital/Zoonar GmbH), 126 (Travelling 10/Hybrid Images/Image Source Salsa); Oxford University Press\Corbis pp.17 (Bianca), 122 (vegetables), 123 (fast food); Oxford University Press\Photodisc p.22 (25 cents); Oxford University Press\DAJ p.122 (tea); Oxford University Press\Photolibrary pp.8 (1), 22 (25 cents), 122 (eggs), 124 (doctor); Oxford University Press\Shutterstock pp.18 (picture frame/pixelheadphoto digitalskillet), 27 (houses/Ewelina Wachala), 41 (Japanese food/bonshan), 119 (newspaper), 122 (salad/Kuttelvaserova Stuchelova); REX/Shutterstock pp.19 (D/Pablo Martinez Monsivais/AP), 121 (Adjectives 7/Image Broker); Shutterstock pp.8 (3/bezikus), (back view couple/Kamenetskiy Konstantin), (wall/rangizzz), (pavement/donatas1205), (poster graphic/balabolka), 9 (6/Vereshchagin Dmitry), (8/Scharfsinn), (9/Lev Kropotov), 10 (1/Jordan Tan), (2/chrisdorney), (3/Marija Stojkovic), (4/Claudio Divizia), (5/Stephen Coburn), (7/Sergio Monti Photography), (8/Jack Jelly), 13 (2/Waldemar Dabrowski), (3/Dawid Lech), 16 (chair/Just2shutter), 17 (Jacek/LightField Studios), 18 (book/Amero), (semi-closed laptop/Peter Kotoff), (phone/RikoBest), (smiling woman/Kim Diaz), (open laptop/Nata-Lia), (three umbrellas/Anton-Burakov), 19 (B/Atstock Productions), (C/stockfour), (1/natushm), (2/Brilliance stock), (3/Nitikorn Poonsiri), (4/David Baumgartner), (5/alexialex), (6/kozirsky), (7/Jakraphong Photography), (8/Claudio Divizia), (9/mrkornflakes), (10/akiyoko), (11/aPhoenixPhotographer), 20 (football shirt/Rabilbanimilbu), 24 (boy/list), (girl/list), (man/list), (woman/list), 26 (car logos/Rose Carson), (Audi TT/eans), 27 (cities/segawa7), (food/Onchira Wongsiri), (restaurants/SPhoto), (books/Billion Photos), (dogs/InBetweentheBlinks), (photos/bepsy), 28 (umbrella/burnel1), (credit card/yablueko), (key/Winai Tepsuttinun), (cap/Etaphop photo), (teddy/Num LPPhoto), 30 (sandwich/gowithstock), (eggs/Africa Studio), (tea/M. Unal Ozmen), (cheese/Nattika), (orange juice/Africa Studio), (Marta/Kudryashova Alla), (Paulo/LightField Studios), (Rob/Azovtsev Maksym), (coffee cup/3DMAVR), 34 (clock graphic 1–6/Lightkite), 36 (2/wavebreakmedia), 37 (Antonio/David Tadevosian), (Charlotte/Africa Studio), (nurse/Monkey Business Images), (hospital background/Joachim Heng), 38 (avocado/NatashaPhoto), (bath/stocksolutions), 40 (water/Gyvafoto), (sugar/Sea Wave), (milk/Jon Le-Bon), (cheese), 78 (1/Ratthaphong Ekariyasap), (8/Brent Hofacker), (10 Rolex/jeafish Ping), 79 (clocks/Lightkite), 81 (charger/Passakorn sakulphan), (purse/A N D A), (iPad/nixki), (Canadian passports/dennizn), 82 (1/Ratthaphong Ekariyasap), (8), (10 Rolex/list), 83 (clocks/Lightkite), 117 (1/Mark Schwettmann), (11/vvoe), (12/Sean Pavone), (14/Luciano Mortula), (15/Critterbiz), 119 (Hungarian passport/Abihatsira Issac), (charger/Ruslan Ivantsov), 120 (People 3/Nadino), (People 4/magedb.com), (People 5/Andresr), (Family 9-10/wavebreakmedia), 121 (Colours 1/Elnur), (Colours 2/Pabkov), (Colours 4/Yganko), (Colours 5/Evgen3dstudio), (Adjectives 1/pics721), (Adjectives 3/jannoon028), (Adjectives 4/SmileStudio), (Adjectives 11/Natasha Kramskaya), (Adjectives 12/Yuralaits Albert), (Adjectives 13/

panpote), (Adjectives 14/psirob), 122 (fish/HLPhoto), (meat/Valentyn Volkov), (pasta/chrisbrignell), (rice/leungchopan), (potatoes/isak55), (fruit/Africa Studio), (bread/Tim UR), (butter/Photographee.eu), (cheese/Tim UR), (sugar/GayvoronskayaYana), (cereal/Oliver Hoffmann), (chocolate/Yeko Photo Studio), (coffee/Artem and Olga Sapegin), (wine/lenetstan), (beer/Tarasyuk Igor), (woman eating/159877448), 124 (teacher/wavebreakmedia), (waiters/Dmitry Kalinovsky), (street with police/Dutourdumonde Photography).

Pronunciation chart artwork by: Ellis Nadler

Illustrations by: Amber Day/Illustration Ltd. pp.12, 13, 36; Stephen Collins p.125; Clementine Hope/NB.Illustration Ltd. p.14 (illustrated background); Laura Perez/Anna Goodson Illustration Agency pp.32–33; Claire Rollet pp.21 (illustrated background), 79; Ben Swift/NB.Illustration Ltd. p.26 (illustrated background); John Haslam pp.92, 93, 94, 96, 97, 98, 99, 100, 101, 102, 118.

Commissioned photography by: Gareth Boden pp.24, 25 (family); MM Studios pp.6, 7, 14 (people), 20 (stallholder), 21 (people), 25 (Jane, Marina and card), 26 (people), 30 (breakfasts for Marta, Paulo and Sakura), 81, 86 (breakfast), 119 (Hungarian ID card), 123 (study); Oxford University Press video stills pp.11, 15, 20 (stall holder), 17 (vox pops), 22 (menu), 23, 27 (Beaulieu), 29 (vox pops), 34 (Rob and Alan), 35 (Jenny and Amy), 39, 41 (vox pops).

Workbook

The publisher would like to thank the following for their permission to reproduce photographs: Alamy pp.6 (American woman/Golden Pixels LLC), 8 (NBA/Grzegorz Knec, JFK/Patti McConville, ET/AF archive), 14 (newspaper/Clynt Garnham Publishing), 15 (ID card/Dinodia Photos), 18 (5p/Studioshots, £10/Tades Yee), 23 (Ben Molyneux Spanish Collection), 26 (Lucas/Julio Bulnes), 31 (3/Hero Images Inc., 7/Robert Convery); Getty Images pp.6 (vase/Heritage Images), 9, 26 (café), 32 (Peter Dazeley); Oxford University Press pp.6 (Brazil, England, cheese), 8 (whiteboard, laptop, pen, door, chair, window, dictionary), 10 (all), 14 (wallet, watch, umbrella, bag, glasses, photo frame, credit card, ID card, tablet), 15 (dictionary, keys, frame, pens, door, table, coats), 24 (all crossword food), 29 (1, 2, 3, 5); Shutterstock pp.6 (Mexico/Rui Vale Sousa, Japan/Vincent St. Thomas, China/Zhao Jian Kang, Spain/Kavalenkau, Italian woman/Izabela Magier, Manuel Neuer/Dmytro Larin, sugar skull/BestStockFoto, Japanese woman/takayuki, Javier Bardem/Andrea Raffin), 8 (ID badge/Paul Paladin, SOS/Choi Jae Young, table/Kaspars Grinvalds, rucksack/Rusly95, coat/photo25th, paper/Peter Kotoff), 12 (women/Antonio Guillem, woman on phone/Antonio Guillem, man on phone/fizkes), 14 (passport/Simon Greig, camera/Billion Photos, notebook/Vitaly Korovin, phone/Nemanja Zotovic, pencil/Sarawut Aiemsinsuk, key/Ilya Akinshin), 16 (cap/Pixfiction, keyring/Alicja Neumiler, plate/Seregam, teddy/Jesus Cervantes, mug/windu, scarf/Yury Gulakov, t-shirt/Surrphoto, football top/ESB Professional), 18 (one US cent/NY-P, $100 note/Chones, 20 euro cent/jooh, £50 note/Chones), 24 (top man/ESB Professional, man in hat/mimagephotography, woman with glasses/WAYHOME studio, bottom woman/WAYHOME studio), 25 (Amelie/El Nariz, Laszlo/CebotariN, children/Evgeny Atamanenko), 29 (4/mimagephotography), 30 (Amy/WAYHOME studio, Luis/mimagephotography, Kate/Charles T. Bennett), 31 (1/michaeljung, 2/Monkey Business Images, 4/Kzenon, 5/ESB Professional, 6/Africa Studio, 7/Africa Studio, 8/GaudiLab, 9/StockLite), 33 (Diego/wavebreakmedia, Jen/Monkey Business Images).

Illustrations by: Mark Duffin pp.24 (meals), 28; Atushi Hara/Dutch Uncle pp.32; Sean Longcroft pp.20 (ex 2), 27; Roger Penwill pp.4, 5, 16, 17, 20 (ex 1), 22.